PNEUMATOLOGY OR THE DOCTRINE OF THE WORK OF THE HOLY SPIRIT.

Works of Revere Franklin Weidner

PNEUMATOLOGY, OR THE DOCTRINE OF THE HOLY SPIRIT
REVERE FRANKLIN WEIDNER

Just & Sinner
425 East Lincoln Ave.
Watseka, IL 60970

www.JustandSinner.com

ISBN 10: **0692612645**
ISBN 13: **978-0692612644**

TABLE OF CONTENTS

INTRODUCTION

Revere Franklin Weidner is one of the brightest lights in American Lutheranism, although he remains relatively unknown in the present day. In addition to being a vastly prolific writer, he wrote books concerning virtually every theological discipline. He has a multi-volume Dogmatics series, several Biblical commentaries, and two volumes on the Biblical Theology of the Old and New Testaments. Weidner also wrote in the areas of ethics, historical theology, and practical theology.

When one reads the works of Weidner, it becomes quickly apparent that he did not seek to be an original thinker. Rather, Weidner desired to bring historic Confessional Lutheran Theology, in the vein of the seventeenth century dogmaticians, to nineteenth century America. Thus, his works are largely summaries of the older dogmaticians. Weidner also drew on contemporary writers, from Lutheran and other church traditions. He is most highly indebted to his eminent teacher Charles Porterfield Krauth, and the German theologian Ernst Luthardt. He rarely takes credit for his own ideas, and often attributes them to the lectures of Krauth.

Of the theologians of the Confessional revival in America of the nineteenth and early twentieth century, many important figures remain unknown. Aside from C.F.W. Walther, Franz Pieper, Wilhelm Loehe, and Charles Krauth, most of these writers have been lost in the annuls of history.

Of the many great figures that characterized this rich period of theological development, Weidner is perhaps the most prolific. Thus, this series is an attempt to bring the name of this significant theologian back into contemporary theological conversations.

We live in an era where scholastic Lutheranism has been largely forgotten due to the influence of later twentieth century theological development. These developments sought to go back to the writings of Luther himself, while ignoring seventeenth century interpretation of those writings. Within this school of thought, prominent in the "Radical Lutheran" school of Gerhard Forde and Steven Paulson, it is argued that there is a profound discontinuity between Luther's Gospel-centric theology and the dry scholasticism of the seventeenth century. In contrast to this, dogmatic theology can rightly be seen as the natural outgrowth and systematizing of Luther's own theological system. While Luther himself was no systematic theologian, he applauded the efforts of Melanchthon for putting Reformation theology within a Dogmatic framework. Now, in the twenty-first century, we are placed in a theological quandary: shall we abandon the Lutheran heritage in favor of newer theological schools of thought which seek to go back to the "real Luther," or should we recapture our rich dogmatic heritage? This series is an attempt to give an answer to this dilemma by providing theological texts which speak just as profoundly to the world and the church's problems in the twenty-first century as they did at the end of the nineteenth. May Weidner's words help the church to "grow in the grace and the knowledge of our Lord and Savior Jesus Christ" (2 Pet. 3:18).

THE APPROPRIATION OF THE FELLOWSHIP OF GOD RESTORED IN CHRIST JESUS.

The Appropriation of this Fellowship may be discussed under two general headings,

1) The Personal Appropriation of Salvation, which will be discussed under the Work of the Holy Spirit, and to which this volume is devoted, and

2) The means which God uses to bestow this Salvation, which will be treated of under the topic of the Church in general, in following volumes.

The Arrangement of the Material.

The dogmatic topics discussed under this subject were not fully developed until the time of our later Dogmaticians. They were not arranged until the time of Calovius (d. 1686), and from the time of Quenstedt (d. 1688), the topics were embraced under the head: The Grace of the Holy Spirit in the Application of Redemption.

Hollaz (d. 1713) says: "The acts of applying Grace, according to the order in which they cohere, and follow one another, are the call, illumination, conversion, regeneration, justification, mystical union with the Triune God, renovation, preservation of faith and holiness, and glorification."

You notice that Hollaz uses the word regeneration in its wider sense. In this enumeration nearly all our later Dogmaticians agree. Hollaz thus vindicates this arrangement: "This order, and, as it were, concatenated series of acts of applying grace, we learn from Acts 26: 17, where Christ says to Paul, 'I send thee to the Gentiles'; behold the grace of the call! 'to open their eyes'; behold the illumination! 'that they may turn from darkness to light'; behold the act of conversion! 'and from the power of Satan unto God'; behold regeneration itself, through which we become the sons of God! 'that they may receive remission of sins?; behold justification! 'and an inheritance among them that are sanctified by faith in me'; behold union with Christ by faith, sanctification, the preservation of holiness, and glorification!"

The doctrine of the Church, as the fellowship of Salvation, and of the means of grace as the medium of the saving activity of the Church, connects itself with this doctrine of the personal application or appropriation of Salvation.

I. THE GRACE OF THE HOLY SPIRIT.

The subjective appropriation of the fellowship of God historically actualized in the salvation wrought by Christ Jesus, is an act of the free Grace of God through the operation of the Holy Spirit who by His prevenient and renewing operations on the internal life of man adapts and determines his will to the acceptance of salvation.

The Scripture doctrine.
Grace, corresponding with the Greek: *charis,* is the free favor of God (the Grace of the Father) towards sinners. It forms the basis of the whole work of redemption:

> Eph. 1: 6, 7, "To the praise of the glory of His grace, which He freely bestowed on us in the Beloved: in whom we have our redemption through His blood, the forgiveness of our trespasses, according to the riches of His grace"

It is made manifest in the sending, and the saving work of Jesus (the Grace of the Son),

> John 1:14, 16, "And the Word became flesh, and dwelt among us. . . full of grace and truth."

For of His fullness we all received, and grace for grace.

> Eph. 2: 7, "That in the ages to come he might show the exceeding riches of his grace in kindness toward us in Christ Jesus: for by grace have ye been saved through faith. Tit. 2:11, "For the grace of God bath appeared, bringing salvation to all man";

Grace is the active principle of the application or appropriation of salvation (the Grace of the Holy Spirit), inasmuch as through grace we become God's children, are justified and saved. The condition of the redeemed is consequently a condition of grace,

> Rom. 5: 2, "Through whom also we have had our access by faith into this grace wherein we stand";
> 1 Pet. 2: 10, "Which in time past were no people, but now are the people of God: which had not obtained mercy, but now have obtained mercy."

This grace consequently stands in antithesis both to man's own merit and work,

> Rom. 4: 4, "Now to him that worketh, the reward is not reckoned as of grace, but as of debt";
> Rom. 4: 16; "For this cause it is of faith, that it may be according to grace";
> Rom. 11: 6, "But if it is by grace, it is no more of works: otherwise grace is no more grace";

and it stands in antithesis also to man's sin and corruption,

> Rom. 5: 15, "For if by the trespass of the one, the many died, much more did the grace of God, and the gif t by the grace of the one man, Jesus Christ, abound unto the many";
> Rom. 5: 20, "But where sin abounded, grace did abound more exceedingly: that, as sin reigned in death, even so might grace reign through righteousness unto eternal life through Jesus Christ our Lord";
> Eph. 2: 3-5, "But God, being rich in mercy, for his great love wherewith he loved us, even when we were dead through our trespasses, quickened us together with Christ (by grace have ye been saved)."

The grace of the appropriation, or the application of salvation, is the grace of the Holy Spirit, for He is the applying agent. In the specific New Testament sense as the applier of the salvation of Christ, the Holy Spirit is the distinctive gift of the New Testament era,

John 7: 39, "For the spirit was not yet given; because Jesus was not yet glorified";

John 14: 26, "But the Comforter, even the Holy Spirit, whom the Father will send in my name, he shall teach you all things, and bring to your remembrance all that I said unto you";

16:7, "It is expedient for you that I go away: For if I go not away, the Comforter will not come unto you; but if I go, I will send him unto you."

Hence He is spoken of as in the service of Christ,

John 15: 26, "But when the Comforter is come whom I will send unto you from the Father, even the Spirit of truth, who proceedeth from the Father, He shall bear witness of me" John 16: 13-15;

and as the Spirit of Christ imparted and sent by Christ,

John 20: 22, "And when he had Said this, he breathed on them, and saith unto them, Receive ye the Holy Ghost";

and is regarded by the apostles themselves as something new, the divine principle of their new life,

Acts,19: 21, "Did ye receive the Holy Ghost when ye believed?";

Rom. 8: 2, "For the law of the Spirit of life in Christ Jesus made us free from the law of sin and of death";

1 John 3: 24, "And hereby we know that He abideth in us by the Spirit which He gave us."

The Church Doctrine.

The history of the doctrine of Grace coheres with that of free will. The Greek Church looked upon grace rather as the aid to human freedom, than as the new creative principle of the inner life. Pelagius represented the same tendency in the Church of the West. Augustine is the great representative of the deeper view, and with the Augustinian theology, excepting his figment of irresistible and particular grace, the Lutheran Church concurs.

In relation to the human will and works the acts of grace are expressed as prevenient grace; preparing, operating, co-operating and preserving grace.

The leading features of the grace of the Holy Spirit are well stated in the exposition of the Third Article of the Creed in Luther's Small Catechism, "the Holy Ghost has called me through the Gospel, enlightened me by His gifts, and sanctified and preserved me in the true faith; in like manner as He calls, gathers, enlightens, and sanctifies the whole Christian Church on earth, and preserves it in union with Jesus Christ in the true faith."

In the Formula of Concord (Sol. Decl. II. 50), the arrangement is this: "God has seen fit through the Word and the right use of the sacraments to call men to eternal salvation, to draw them to Himself, to convert, regenerate, and sanctify them."

The various grades, vocation, illumination, conversion, regeneration, justification, mystical union, renovation, sanctification, are not so much to be separated as if they were divided in time, as separated in the order of nature and of thought. Great practical confusion arises from the attempt to separate actually and divide appreciably from one another those great acts which indeed have an order of succession but are simultaneous things.

Definition of the Dogmaticians.
Grace.
Hollaz: "The applying grace of the Holy Spirit is the source of those divine acts by which the Holy Spirit, through the Word of God and the Sacraments, dispenses, offers to us, bestows and seals the spiritual and eternal favors designed for man by the great mercy of God the Father, and procured by the fraternal redemption of Jesus Christ."

Prevenient Grace.
Baier: "By prevenient grace is understood the divine inspiration of the first holy thought and godly desire. This grace is called prevenient, because it is prior to our deliberate consent or because in this way the will of the person to be converted is anticipated."

Hollaz: "Prevenient grace is that act, wherein the Holy Spirit offers to man, dead in sin, the benevolence of the Father and the merit of Christ through the Word of God, takes away his natural incapacity, and invites, excites, impels, and urges him to repentance."

Preparing Grace.
Hollaz: "Preparing grace is that act, wherein the Holy Spirit overcomes the natural and actual resistance, imbues the mind with a knowledge of the letter of the Gospel, and softens the will by the Word of the Law, that it may be more and more disposed to the reception of saving faith."

Operating Grace.
Hollaz: "Operating grace, as a special term, designates that act of grace by which the Holy Spirit confers the power of believing and justifying faith. To it belong regeneration, justification and mystical union."

Co-operating Grace.
Hollaz: "Co-operating grace is that act of grace wherein the Holy Spirit acts concurrently with the justified man to sanctification, and the bringing forth of good works. To this belongs renovation."

Preserving Grace.
Hollaz: "Preserving grace is that act by which the Holy Spirit, dwelling in justified and renewed men, defends them by supernatural strength against the temptations of the devil, the world, and the flesh, which solicit to sin and apostasy from God, and sustains and increases their faith and holiness, that they may not fall from grace, but persevere in it and be eternally saved."

Glorifying Grace.
Hollaz: "Glorifying grace is that act by which God transfers those who are justified, and who remain faithful unto death, from the kingdom of grace to the kingdom of glory, that they may obtain eternal happiness and praise God eternally."

Assisting and Indwelling Grace.
Quenstedt divided grace into assisting grace, which acts exterior to man, and indwelling grace, which enters the heart of man and changing it spiritually, inhabits it. To the assisting grace belong prevenient grace, exciting grace, operating grace and perfecting

grace, of which the first three operate as preparatory acts, but by perfecting grace the act of real conversion is accomplished. Indwelling grace occurs only after conversion, in sanctification.

"The grace of God acts before conversion, in it, and after it." Before conversion the acts of grace are called prevenient, preparative, and exciting; in conversion we can speak of operating and completing grace; after conversion the acts of grace are co-operative, assisting, and completing.

Effects of the Working of Grace.
Quenstedt: "Grace, effecting and completing conversion by means of the Word, produces (1) The knowledge of sin, which is the first stage of conversion; (2) Compunction of heart, that there may be detestation of sins committed and grief on their account; (3) The act of faith itself and confidence in Christ."

The four-fold Office of the Grace of the Holy Spirit.
Our later dogmaticians have ascribed to the Holy Ghost a four-fold office.

(1) *Officium elenchticum*, or convicting office,
John 16: 8, "And He when He is come, will convict the world in respect of sin, and of righteousness, and of judgment";

(2) *Officium didascalicum*, or teaching office,
John 16: 13-15, "Howbeit when He, the Spirit of truth, is come, He shall guide you unto all the truth...and He shall declare unto you the things that are to come...He shall take of mine, and shall declare it unto you";

(3) *Officium paedeuticum*, or correcting office,
2 Tim. 3: 16, "Every scripture is inspired of God and is profitable for teaching, for reproof, for correction, for instruction, which is in righteousness"; Rom. 8: 14, "For as many as are led by the Spirit of God, these are the sons of God";

(4) *Officium paracleticum*, or comforting office,
Rom. 8: 26, "And in like manner the Spirit also helpeth our infirmity: for we know not how to pray as we ought; but the Spirit Himself maketh intercession f or us with groanings which cannot be uttered."

Later Development.
Mysticism.

Mysticism sets forth a three-fold way of grace: (1) purification, (2) illumination, (3) union. In the true order illumination precedes both the others. The illumination and regeneration of the sinner do not take place by the purgation or abstraction of the soul from created objects, and the Holy Spirit does not immediately, but by means of the divine Word, enlighten us, II Pet. 1: 18, 19.

Rationalism.

Rationalism denied the supernatural operations of grace and substitutes for them man's own moral power which is aroused and strengthened by instructive moral teaching. Supernaturalism rose above rationalism without reaching the true view that grace is in a strictly specific sense, the divinely creative power of the new spiritual life.

II. CALLING OR VOCATION.

With the annunciation of the grace of God in Christ the calling Word of the Holy Spirit directs itself to the souls of men, in order by the illumination and awakening operation which it exercises to render possible to all to whom it is set forth, that faith which appropriates salvation.

The Scripture Doctrine.
The placing of the calling or vocation in the front rank rests upon the character of the divine Word as the essential form in which God reveals Himself and brings effectually nigh to man His gracious will. The evidence of this is found in the whole course of the history of salvation, with which correspond the acts of our Lord.

He first of all calls men to the kingdom of heaven, calls them to become His followers. To the fishermen of Galilee, He calls, "Come ye after Me, and I will make you fishers of men"; the call contemplating their own spiritual life as well as their vocation as teachers, Matt. 4: 19-21. He calls, "Come, and ye shall see," John 1: 39; He declares, "Come not to call the righteous, but sinners to repentance," Matt. 9: 13; Luke 5: 32. He calls, "Come unto Me, all ye that labor and are heavy laden, and I will give you rest," Matt. 11: 28. The privileges of the kingdom are represented under the image of a great supper or of a marriage feast, to which a call in the form of an invitation is given, Luke 14: 16; Matt. 22: 3, 14. The invited are denominated the called. When His people are represented as a flock; it is not a flock driven by the shepherd, but a flock drawn by His voice and guided by His call. The sheep hear Him; He calls His own sheep by name; and the whole work of our Lord in gathering the Church, is regarded as His calling of the sheep, John 10: 3-16.

The same idea develops itself in the ministry and teaching of the Apostles. Christians are constantly designed by St. Paul as the called, "called to be Jesus Christ's"; "called to be saints"; Rom. 1: 6-7; 1 Cor. 1:2; etc.; they are styled, "the called according to the purpose of God," Rom. 8: 28.

God's activity in our salvation is set forth as a calling, "them He also called; and whom He called, them He also justified," Rom. 8:30; "God is faithful, through whom ye were called into the fellowship of His Son Jesus Christ our Lord," 1 Cor. 1; 9; 7: 15, 11; Gal. 1: 6, 15; 5: 8, 13; Eph. 4: 1, 4; Col. 3: 15; 1Thess. 2: 12; 4: 7; 5: 24: 2 Thess. 2: 14.

In 1 Tim. 6: 12 we read that Timothy was called to life eternal. In 2 Tim. 1: 9 we learn that believers are called with a holy calling, because it proceeds from God, and is opposed to the sinful condition of man, and in 1 Pet. 1: 15; 2: 9; we read that we are called "out of darkness into the marvelous light of God"; and in 1 Pet. 3: 9 that, "hereunto were we called, that we should inherit a blessing," that "we might receive the promise of the eternal inheritance," Heb. 9: 15.

To man this call is earnest and urgent. The order is, "constrain them to come in" Luke 14; 23, i.e. put forth that earnestness in the name of God which shall exercise the mightiest constraint, which the human soul is capable of receiving, without violence to that liberty in which is involved its responsibility. It is connected with urgency as regards time; it is an urgency which never says tomorrow; but always today. "Today if ye shall hear His voice, harden not your heart," Heb. 3: 7, 8. Hence the vocation is considered as deciding the condition of him to whom it comes in vain; he that is called, and finally refuses, is lost, Luke 14: 24. It is represented as something which men may put from them: selves, which they are responsible for putting from them- selves, Acts 13: 46; Rom. 10: 16, 21. The result of this casting off of the Word is represented as fatal, followed by blindness and hardness and reprobation, John 12: 40 (in connection with verse 37); 2 Cor. 2:16.

This vocation of God, contemplated in its generic aspect, is designed for the whole race, for all nations, Matt. 28: 19; Mark 16: 15; Luke 34: 46, 47. Still more minute is its application. It is said, "Preach the Gospel to the whole creation," Mark 16: 15.

This vocation in its actual historic importation to men has not been instantaneous, but follows the law of universal history. It has been gradual, Rom. 11: 31. In the position of the world which is destitute of revelation, the providence and general testimony of

God to Himself, prepared the way for the vocation, Acts 14: 17; 17: 27; Rom. 1: 19, 20; Rom. 2: 15.

The Church Doctrine.
Definition of Call or Vocation.
Hollaz: "Calling to the kingdom of Christ is that act of grace, by which the Holy Spirit manifests to men, outside of the church, through the divine Word, the will of God in regard to the salvation of sinners, and offers to them the benefits purchased by Christ the Redeemer, that they may be brought to the Church, may be converted and may obtain eternal salvation."

Remarks on Luthardt's Criticism.
This definition is objected to by Luthardt as too narrow, inasmuch as calling pertains also to those who have been born and baptized in the Church. But the definition of Hollaz may be justified, even if by the *ecclesia* or the Church, he means the visible Church. Then his definition refers to the primary call, to those who are not of that visible church, which is undoubtedly the aspect in which the call is frequently contemplated in the New Testament. The call to Pagans was a call to men outside of the Church; and the call to the Jews was. a call to men outside of the Christian Church.

Or if he refers to the invisible Church, the Church strictly so called, the Church of living believers and true saints, he does not exclude the idea, that those who are baptized also need the call, if they have not been faithful to their baptismal covenant. He defines, moreover, not simply *vocatio,* but *vocatio ad regnum Christi,* calling unto the kingdom of Christ.

Definition of Pedagogic and General or Indirect Call.
This distinction has been made since the time of Quenstedt (d. 1688). Hollaz (d. 1713) takes as a basis for his definition this general pedagogic and indirect vocation.

> Acts 14: 17; 17: 25-27, "And yet He left not Himself without witness, in that He did good, and gave you from heaven rains and fruitful seasons, filling your hearts with food and gladness";

Rom. 2: 4, "Or despisest thou the riches of His goodness and forbearance and long-suffering, not knowing that the goodness of God leadeth thee to repentance?"

He defines the general or indirect call thus: "It is that by which God more obscurely and as it were from afar invites and brings to the gate of the Church, sinners who are outside of the Church so that they are thereby led to seek for the true worship of God and His Church. This He does (a) objectively, by the revelation of His government and by the divine beneficence towards His creatures; (b) effectively, by an efficacious influence and divine impulse by which alike from innate theoretical and practical ideas and from the tokens of divine beneficence... practical suggestions and conclusions are aroused in the minds of the unbelieving, though in an unequal degree, so that they search out the true worship of God; (c) cumulatively, by the growing report concerning the Church which is spread throughout the whole world."

By this indirect vocation is excited a certain penitence and aversion towards sin, which though in no degree a substitute for grace, prepares the mind of man for a higher degree of it.

Definition of the Special or Direct Call.
But calling, in the proper sense of the word, is the special call, the direct call. This is either ordinary or extraordinary. The ordinary is through the preaching and teaching of the divine Word. The extraordinary is that which departs from the ordinary means, and is divided by the old divines into immediate and mediate. The immediate is that in which God calls men without means, in His own immediate person, as He called Abraham and Paul. The mediate is that in which he employs extraordinary media or means such as miracles and similar modes of reaching man, as the appearing of Jonah to the Ninevites, the star which called and guided the Magi.

Lutheranism and Calvinism Contrasted.
The old predestinarian theory was compelled to acknowledge that in some sense the call was represented as something universal. But it evades the proper inherence by various subtle and insufficient distinctions in regard to the will of God.

In opposition to the doctrine of absolute predestination, the Lutheran Theologians characterized the vocation 1) as serious, 2) as efficacious, or as bearing real divine force and efficacy, and 3) as universal, meant for all.

1) The vocation is serious. God is in earnest, He means it. The words of vocation do not mean less than their sound, but in consequence of the very imperfection of language, the meaning, when they convey a divine call, is more than their sound. If the earnest call of a father to a wandering child to come, means come, then does the call of God, equally serious, yet more urgently mean, come. It is not as Calvin teaches, merely the manifestation by sign and command, but it arises out of the deepest purpose and good pleasure of God who seriously desires the saving illumination and conversion of all men.

2) It is efficacious. It is accompanied by an actual divine working sufficient in itself to its ends. Power goes with the Word.

Calvinism holds that the Word has not bound up in it the divine power which makes it efficacious, but that it needs in each case a co-working of God's Spirit to render it efficacious, and that this co-working is separable from it and only accompanies it in the case of the elect. This view involves a complete dualism and destroys the character of the Word as a real means of grace. Grace does not go in, with and by it, but only at most and at best simultaneously with it, and in most cases does not go with it at all.

Quenstedt thus defines the form of vocation: "It consists in a manifestation of the divine will and an offering of the benefits acquired by Christ: a manifestation which is serious and in the intent of God, always sufficient and always efficacious." He proves that it is serious from Matt. 23: 37, "O Jerusalem, Jerusalem which killeth the prophets, and stoneth them that are sent unto her." Although it falls short of its effects, it is hindered by men presenting an obstacle, and thus becomes inefficacious by fault of the evil and obstinate will of man.

In antithesis to the Calvinists, Quenstedt says: "The Calvinists distinguish between the external and internal vocation, and represent them as differing in three respects a) with respect to their principles or sources, the external is given through the ministry of the Word, the internal is given through the Holy Spirit inwardly, illuminating the heart; b) with respect to the subjects or persons recipient, the external is common to the elect and reprobate, the internal is peculiar to the elect alone; c) with respect to the efficacy, the internal vocation alone is efficacious and irresistible.

"We admit that a distinction exists, but we do not oppose the external vocation to the internal, nor do we separate the one from the other, inasmuch as the external vocation is the medium and organ of the internal, and through the external God is efficacious in the hearts of men. If the external vocation did not exactly accord with the internal, it would be vain, fallacious, deceptive."

The Calvinistic dualism here arises from the false theory of predestination. It really robs the external vocation of all true character as a divine medium of grace and simply embarrasses the work of salvation with a useless element.

3) It is universal. In affirming that the divine gracious will is as universal as the corruption of mankind; the old theologians laid the premise of their inference that vocation as the actualizing, or putting into effect of that gracious will, is universal all men are called, and every man is called.

Quenstedt: "The vocation is universal in two respects, 1) the object of vocation is to all men, without exception, as respect the divine intention,

> 1 Tim. 2: 4, "Who willeth that all men should be saved, and come to the knowledge of the truth";
> 2 Pet. 3: 9, "The Lord is not willing that any should perish, but that all should come to repentance."

"It is universal in view of the actual execution of the calling at some period, to all men."

The Universal Call Given at Three Periods.

This universal vocation is said to have been given at three periods, 1) in the time of our first parents alter the fall, Gen. 3: 8, 9, 15; 2) in the time of Noah after the flood, Gen. 9: 9-12; 3) in the time of the apostles, Mark 16: 15, 20; Rom. 10: 18; Col. 1: 6, 23.

In proving the universality of the apostolic setting forth of the Gospel, the epigrammatic sentence is added, that where the apostle did not come, the epistle came. It has been said that the vocation demands oral announcement. This is true etymologically, but not in fact. A vocation can be mediated by letter as well as by voice, and a blind man can receive vocation at the tips of his fingers as the deaf man can receive vocation with his eyes.

It may not be easy or possible to demonstrate that every part of the race has been reached by voice or letter, but the whole of our race certainly has been approached at some period with at least a general vocation.

The True Solution Suggested.
The true solution of the difficulty is found in separating between men considered in a mass and men considered individually and separately, to distinguish between a vocation universally given and a vocation universally received. An invitation may be universal in its terms, though many for whom it is meant, never hear of it. To make a vocation universally and separately received, it would be necessary to show not only that at some time the existing race had been called, but that each individual in every race had been so called, which no one pretends is the case. The call is meant for every human creature; it has come at some period to the great representative masses of mankind; and, if the race had been as faithful to the duty of receiving and transmitting the vocation as God has been earnest in giving it, the whole world would have received it. We must stand by the divine declaration in regard to it, whatever may be the mystery of the actual course of the divine vocation in the world.

Quenstedt labors to show that the apostolic teaching reached even to America, and there are some remarkable facts brought out by modern research, which seem to show that before the advent of Europeans, subsequent to the discovery of America by Columbus, there had been on this continent points of connection with ancient Christian teaching, not to mention the fact that distinguished writers have found in our Indians remnants of the lost tribes of Israel, still retaining many of the religious ideas of the Israelitish race. (Prescott, Conquest of Mexico and Peru.)

Testimony of Hollaz.
With this universality of purpose is connected the possibility of its being given to all.

Hollaz: "When we assert that vocation to the kingdom of God is universal we do not mean to say that to all and each of men actually and directly, through preachers especially sent, the doctrine of the Gospel has been. announced, but that God, most merciful, has so clearly promulgated the Gospel doctrine concerning the obtaining salvation through faith in Christ, that all men whatsoever can attain to the knowledge of it, so that God bas denied, by an absolute decree, to no nation, to no individual, an opportunity of knowing of that doctrine and the way by which it is possible to obtain a knowledge of it."

Why Some Nations are Destitute of the Gospel.
That there actually are and have been many nations destitute of the Gospel is accounted for by several considerations. One is their own earlier guilt. Hollaz: "That nations formerly and yet in our own day and many people, are destitute of the preaching of the Word, is their own fault, not the fault of a fixed will or counsel of God; absolutely denying them the light of the Gospel; for 1) these nations despise and maliciously reject the Word of God; 2) that vocation and idea concerning Christian doctrine and ceremonies, in general, which through report is at this day universal, they neglect; 3) the pedagogic effective vocation they do not employ to its proper use, to search out the true worship and the true Church of God; wherefore they deprive themselves, by their own fault, of this salutary vocation which is through the preaching of the Gospel."

This is true as far as is necessary to vindicate God in His dealings; but it is not true in such sense as to, absolve God's people from greater earnestness in the work of evangelizing the world. It may be said, in a word, that God bas put into our world the forces actually necessary to reach the race with his vocation, and that whatever may be the speculative difficulties in harmonizing. the existing facts with the avowal of God as to His own wish; we dare not attenuate or explain away the divine declaration. If any man perish, whatever the solution of the fact may be, the solution is not that God does not desire his salvation.

Statement of Quenstedt.
Quenstedt, in meeting the objection, that the present generation is deprived of the call by the sin of their ancestors, which assumes that the children bear the guilt of their fathers, appeals to the fact

that at least the general report of Christianity and the general or indirect call reaches everyone.

But it is almost demonstrable that such is not the case. There are probably many of our race who have not heard even in a vague and general way of Christianity. Some such there are in the bounds of nominal Christianity. There are parts of Africa, to which, certainly when Quenstedt wrote and probably to this hour, no report of the existence of Christianity has penetrated. But even if we grant that some loose general report in regard to Christianity has reached every man, we can hardly conceive that such imperfect kinds as these would seriously affect the responsibility of men. It is indeed a sad truth that the Christianity of which many of our race seem to know is not such as would draw them to it.

It is easier to believe that God does not give these men a vocation, than that he will consider such a call a vocation, and hold them guilty for not acting on it. The nominal Christians, or rather the people of nominally Christian countries, have often been only the pioneers of the vices and the crimes of a corrupt civilization. To the poor savage, Christianity has sometimes seemed to mean rum, smallpox, pollution and extermination. It is impossible to maintain the theory that every child of man has individually received a salutary vocation. We see here as everywhere that God's world of nature, grace, and civil constitution, is, a historical world, a world of beginning, gradations, growth and slow consummation. The law of the world, from the lowest to the highest development, is conformed to the general principle-first the blade, then the ear, then the full corn in the ear. The kingdom of God is as a mustard seed, which develops by slow, long growth, into a tree. The higher the life the more fixed the law. The kingdom of God is leaven in a measure of meal, which gradually by self-assimilating power, works itself through the mass. The idea of a human being is that of ripened, adult, mental, moral and, physical life. But this idea matures from the germ of being through the stages of infancy and of later life; after long years, it consummates itself in the perfect man.

The movement of salvation like that of the general government of the world is from little to great, and we must be content here to rest in humble faith in God's loving desire, that all men should be saved and come to a knowledge of the truth; leaving to the Infinite One Himself to solve in due time what He alone can solve-why so many seem to be out of the way of salvation and without the means of coming to a knowledge of the truth.

If God had pleasure in the loss of men it would not reveal itself in the loss of some of our race, but in the loss of all. And there is no sound thinking which can accept the proposition that God desires to save one man without resting in the assurance that He desires to save every man. If God's absolute decree is the thing that determines the salvation of man, then Universalism, not Calvinism, is the natural result. And experience has shown that out of high Calvinism, Universalism has actually grown.

III. ILLUMINATION.

The Word of Vocation or Calling applies itself primarily with illumination or light to the consciousness of man, in order to work in him the knowledge of sin and of grace. But it reaches through that consciousness to the will, in order to call forth in the will new motions o! life, which find their ultimate aim in conversion.

The Doctrine of Scripture.
The natural condition of man is frequently represented in the Scripture as darkness in the moral sense out of which we are redeemed by the salvation which is in Christ.

> Luke 1: 79, "Dayspring from on high shall visit us; to give light to them that sit in darkness, and the shadow of death, to guide our feet into the way of peace";
> John 1: 5, "The light shineth in the darkness; and the· darkness apprehended it not";
> 3: 19, "Men loved the darkness rather than the light; for their works were evil";
> Col. 1: 13, "The Father delivered us out of the power of darkness, and translated us into the Kingdom of the Son of His love";
> Acts 26: 18; Rom. 13: 12; Eph. 5: 8; 1 John 2: 8, 9, 11.

Over against this darkness of our natural state, Christ is represented as the light of the world.

> John 8: 12, "I am the light of the world: he that loveth me shall not walk in the darkness, but shall have the light of life"; Luke 2: 32; John 1: 4, 5, 9; 9: 5; 12: 35, 36, 46.

Through the divine witness in the Word there goes forth from Christ a new light into the hearts of men, a light which renders them susceptible to the light, capable of receiving it. Light enables that on which it falls to bear more light; continual light teaches the eye to gaze without being dazzled; for light alone makes us capable of itself; deprived of it long, we are unable to bear it. Light can blind as well as give vision. Men are in the light and walk in the light, by which is indicated a new moral state of life,

> Acts 26: 18, "To turn them from darkness to light";
> Eph. 5: 8, "For ye were once darkness, but are now light in the Lord"; 1 John 1: 7; 2: 8, 9.

With this change of the state of life is consummated a change of the whole mode of thinking, which is the work of the Spirit of God, a great moral process, 1 Cor. 1: 17-2: 16.

The illumination appears also throughout as a preliminary process, an antecedent necessity in the heart, which sheds light on all,

> 2 Cor. 4: 46, "In whom the god of this world hath blinded the minds of the unbelieving, that the light of the Gospel of the glory of Christ, who is the image of God, should not dawn upon them...Seeing it is God, that said, Light shall shine out of darkness, who shined in our hearts, to give the light of the knowledge of the glory of God in the face of Jesus Christ."

He not only calls us by His Word but that Word is one that sheds light on all that He would have us experience and do.

The Church Doctrine.
The Greek Church.
The Greek Church, which loves to apprehend Christianity in its aspects as a new knowledge of truth, designates saving grace and the transfer of man into it by the terms *phos* (light) and *photisma* (illumination); the former used repeatedly in the New Testament in the same general sense and *photisma* having the same force with *photismos*, 2 Cor. 4: 4, 6, in both of which passages illumination would be a better translation than light. See the margin of the Revised Version.

The Greek Fathers were especially wont to call baptism *photisma* so that the two terms are in this respect often treated as synonymous, and indeed this identification of baptism and illumination is very general in the Oriental Church. A similar use is found in the Syriac version of the New Testament, which translates Heb. 6: 4, "those who were once enlightened," as "those who were once baptized"; also in Heb. 10: 32.

Topic not Separately Treated Until the Time of Hollaz.
Our Lutheran dogmaticians employ the illumination to mark one distinct degree in the appropriation of salvation. The Small Catechism separately specifies "enlightened me by His gifts." The Formula of Concord says "the Holy Spirit through the Word preached and heard illuminates and converts the heart so that men can believe in and assent to the Word." Yet in spite this distinction so early marked, with the exception Calvin, who briefly touches upon illumination, the topic has not a special sphere assigned it in the theological systems until the time of Hollaz. The occasion was given to Hollaz by the prevalent Mysticism and the growing tendency of pietism to obscure sound doctrine on this point. This made it the more necessary that it should be separately treated.

Condition of Unilluminated Man.
Hollaz: "In an unilluminated man there is not merely a negative ignorance but also an ignorance of depraved inclination, which is error contrary to true knowledge, because the natural man not only does not receive the things of the Spirit of God, but they are foolishness unto him, 1 Cor. 2: 14. Therefore, not only mere ignorance, but likewise carnal-mindedness (Rom. 8: 6) and the wisdom of this world (1 Cor. 1: 20), are opposed to a saving knowledge. The world has its wisdom, but it is immersed in the darkness of arrogance, so as to array itself against the wisdom of God, 2 Cor. 10: 5."

The Goal of Illumination.
Hollaz: "The light of saving knowledge is its goal. By the Law is the knowledge of sin, Rom. 3: 20. The knowledge of the glorious grace of God, unveiled in the face of Jesus Christ, proceeds from the Gospel, 2 Cor. 4: 6. Assent attends this knowledge, by which man enlightened regards as sure and beyond doubt all that is

revealed in the Word of God, particularly the Gospel message concerning the remission of sins and the eternal salvation to be secured through Christ."

Design of Illumination.
Hollaz: "The first and principal design of illumination is to prepare man for conversion...he is imbibed with a knowledge of God and of sacred things, and illuminated, as if by a light, so that he is prepared to receive justifying grace. The illuminating grace, therefore, precedes the completion of conversion."

Definition of Illumination.
Hollaz: "Illumination is that act of applying grace by which the Holy Spirit teaches sinful man, who has been called to the Church, through the ministry of the Word, and more and more animates him with a sincere desire and purpose, that, the darkness of ignorance and error being dispelled, he may be imbued with a knowledge of the Word of God, and be led by the Law to acknowledge his sins and by the Gospel to see the divine pity which rests on the merit of Christ and thus infuses or instills a knowledge of the same."

Illumination consequently belongs to "preparing grace" and a measure of it precedes complete conversion though it also continues after conversion, taking the term illumination in its widest sense. The illumination which brings us to Christ must precede in the order of thought our coming to Christ; but the whole illumination of the Spirit of God follows us or rather surrounds us at every stage of the divine life. It goes before us in justification, yet the light which goes before us can only guide us as it enters into us. We see no light except that which comes within the mind. We know the light without, by the light within, which corresponds with it. The star which guided the Magi was in the East; but it could only guide them as the light was received by the Magi themselves. This light goes with us and in us in sanctification.

Illumination is Teaching Grace and Anointing Grace.
Hollaz: "Enlightening grace is called teaching grace, because the Holy Spirit, in enlightening, teaches all things necessary to salvation, John 14: 26; likewise anointing grace, from 1 John 2: 20, 27; opening of the eyes of the mind, Acts 26: 18, for as a blind

person obtains the power of seeing by the opening of his eyes, so the sinner, filled with the darkness of ignorance, receives, by the illumination of the Holy Spirit, the power of knowing the true God."

Not Confined to the Regenerate.
It is a mistaken view when Buddeus confines illumination to the regenerate. It is that without which men would not become regenerate. The light of the morning wakens, before it renders the external world visible, and beginning with our conscious day it follows us to its close.

Illumination Legal and Evangelical.
Corresponding with the course and gradations of the new life and the twofold character of the divine Word as Law and Gospel, illumination is twofold. It is legal and evangelical.

Legal illumination manifests to us sin, the wrath of God, and the temporal and external penalties of sin (Rom. 7: 7). It is therefore only pedagogically salutary. It shows us our sickness but cannot go beyond this and restore us to health. It cannot supply our need, yet it does a great work in showing our need to us. The diagnosis of the physician does not cure a patient, but the cure rests on the diagnosis.

Evangelical illumination reveals to us the grace of God founded upon the merit of Christ, the righteousness which avails before God and life everlasting (2 Cor. 4:4). This is completely salutary (Luke 1: 77-79).

Thus the light of the day does the double work of revealing to us perils of the one pathway, and enabling to turn to the other pathway and to journey by it.

The Holy Spirit Illuminates Through Means.
In opposition to the whole tendency of fanaticism, of spurious illumination, of false revelation and the mystical doctrine of ecstasy, our divines constantly teach that the Holy Spirit illumines us not immediately but mediately, not without means but through the means or medium of the divine Word, either in itself or with the sacraments. It is the denial of this doctrine, not always openly or consciously but often virtually, which is the spring of nearly all the prevalent fanaticism.

Men imagine themselves to be illumined and converted by inspiration, and suppose themselves to have new revelation, as the witness that they are born of God.

The so called doctrine of "sensible assurance" which has gone over from Methodism into other parts of the Church, means this. It substitutes the stimulated spirit of man for the Spirit of God, emotion for the testimony of the Word, justification by sensation for justification by faith. In this illumination, this preliminary for conversion, there is secured a work which is moral in its nature, because of the influence of the Word and yet personal in its character, because the presence and energy of the Holy Spirit in His substance and person are in it.

It is not what the work of the Word would be without the Holy Spirit personally energizing, for that would be simply moral and didactic, nor is it what the work of the Holy Spirit would be without the Word, for that would be simply supernatural. It would be in the fullest and most technical sense a miracle. Nothing more essentially miraculous than that which is done without means. It is no more ordinarily to be expected that the miracle of the work of the Spirit should take place on man without means than that the sick should be healed with a touch or the dead raised by a word. God's plan is to bind up the invisible with the visible, to give the heavenly in, with and under the earthly and so the illumination energies of the Spirit are bound up with the external Word.

But our divines do not mean to bind illumination to the single personal act of occupation in hearing or reading the Word. But they say that the power of illumining with which the divine Word is endowed is not precisely bound to the act or time of hearing, reading or meditating, but the Word of God which has been heard or has been read, transmitted into the mind and there retained, possesses always its power of illumination. It may be latent, but its vital force will reveal itself on every occasion which is opened and the divine Word may transmit the forces it generates, as one wave of air or of water seems to lose itself, yet is perpetuated in the remoter waves it calls into being. But the necessary pre supposition to the power always is that men earnestly occupy themselves with the Word. Seeming accident may excite this earnestness, but the earnestness itself is indispensable. God in His benignity seriously desires and intends to illumine all men. But they only are actually illumined, who, being called and brought to the Church, admit the grace of the Holy Spirit and attentively hear, read and meditate on the divine Word.

The Teaching of the Mystics.
The Mystics, e.g. Molinas, Weigel, etc., taught there should be inward stillness. They had various degrees: (1) silence from words; (2) silence from desires; (3) silence from thoughts, and this is what they called the inward Sabbath of the soul.

In antithesis to this, our divines taught that illumination is not to be idly waited for. There is to be no tacit expectation of the light of an immediate divine revelation. So far is it from the truth that a supernatural divine light is to be expected as the result of silence; that on the contrary the outward Word of God which if the purest light is to be seriously preached, seriously heard, frequently read and attentively weighed, and fervent prayers mingled with holy hymns are to be lifted to heaven, that the saving light of knowledge our hearts and may continue to increase.

Not Only the Intellect but also the Will Must be Enlightened.
The operation of illumination extends not merely to the cognitive powers, but to the will. It gives light to the mind, it gives it also to the heart. First immediately, the understanding of the sinner is illumined, 2 Cor. 4: 6, "God shined in our hearts"; Eph. 1: 18, "The eyes of your heart being enlightened." Consequent upon this, and mediated by it, the will of man is enlightened teaches us to deny ungodliness and to correct our evil will, not simply teaching us that this is to be done, but showing us the way to it, Tit. 2: 11, 12.

In the nature of the case, the enlightenment of the intellect precedes that of the will, still it cannot exist independent of it. A true divine illumination of the mind never takes place without an illumination of the will, and herein it is totally different from a merely natural illumination, in which the judgment may be clearly taught the good, and the will tenaciously cling to the bad.

The two are distinct but inseparable. They have a logical sequence, but no chronological one. The divine enlightenment of the one involves that of the other. There may be human illumination of the mind without a saving illumination of the will, but there can be no genuine divine one. The real divine illumination of the mind perfects itself only where there is a corresponding operation of the will. The secret of the Lord is only with them that fear Him.

"If any man willeth to do His will, he shall know of the teaching, whether it be of God," (John 7: 17), i.e. the will which does, is inflexibly related to the mind which knows, inasmuch as the supernatural illumination is a successive act of applying grace. There may be in deed an imperfect illumination in man's understanding, having a divine source in general without the sanctification of man's will.

This can be seen in the case of Balaam, who was enlightened by Jehovah as to His purposes, yet was not divinely illumined. Judas Iscariot was enlightened by our Lord Himself but was not illumined. Men may be so far enlightened as to do wondrous works in the name of Christ, yet so devoid of illumination that at the last day He shall say to them, "I never knew you" (Matt. 7:22) Men may be so enlightened in a knowledge of divine things, naturally acquired, that they may sit in the seat of Moses, or in the seat of the Apostles, and yet be as regards the internal illumination of which we speak, blind guides lacking the true comprehension of the very which they utter. A blind man may teach optics. clothed in the human words the gospel may be as astronomy or grammar is taught. Men may with intellectual eagerness learn divine things, while they resist the divine energy which goes with them, and which would give them true illumination, if they did not resist it. The result is that having eyes they see not, or seeing with the outward eye, they resist the true entrance of the light of God which illuminates the soul. Therefore, all divine illumination of the understanding, naturally leads to the illumination of the will, man may perversely hem in the operation in his intellect so as to prevent its revealing its power in his will. He puts asunder what God has joined together, and renders himself like a man whose nerves bear to his brain the impression from the circumference of sensation, but who has sundered the nerves which transmit the forces of notion from the center outward.

Mysticism would have purification to precede illumination, contrary to the truth, for it is the illumination through which the purification begins. The first result of its entrance is that it shows the impurities; the next is that it helps us in every process of removal; We are not to sweep rooms in the dark. The first step to cleaning is the admission of light.

Imperfect and Perfect Illumination.
The imperfect illumination of which we have been speaking is also, consequently literal and pedagogic.

The perfect illumination, on the other hand, is spiritual and completely saving. The letter of the first we stop at the letter, killeth, the spirit of the second always gives life. The former is to be ascribed to assisting grace, the latter to indwelling grace.

Quenstedt expresses the distinction thus: pedagogic illumination is merely literal and external, when one is instructed in the knowledge of divine truth, and is convinced of its certainty in his conscience, but has not this known truth as yet sealed in his heart, or confirmed by the gracious indwelling of the Holy Spirit; illumination is spiritual, gracious, and internal, when anyone for instance, truly regenerate, not only has a literal understanding of the evangelical doctrine but is at the same time the temple of the Holy Ghost, inhabited graciously by Him."

Hollaz defines them as follows: "The former, imperfect, literal, and pedagogic, is an operation of the Holy Ghost, by which He through His grace outwardly assisting and preparing the understanding of man who is indeed unregenerate, yet tending to regeneration, instructs him with a literal knowledge of the thing to be believed and produces an historical assent to the gospel, so that he is more and more disposed to receive saving faith. The latter, perfect, spiritual, and completely saving, is an operation of the Holy Spirit, whereby He enters the contrite heart of man and dwells in it, kindles a saving knowledge of the mercy of God, which mercy is founded on the merit of Christ, producing a trusting assent to the gospel and confirms and seals trust and. assent by His inward witness."

The former, literal illumination, is also consequently an operation of the Holy Ghost. It is a true operation. It is salutary, inasmuch as it tends to salvation. It is also supernatural, on which account our dogmaticians never divide illumination, properly so-called, into natural and supernatural, for the natural knowledge of God, such as exists apart from this supernatural revelation of Himself, is in consequence of its incompleteness not to be designated illumination, as we here term.

Illumination a Gradual Process.

This illuminating activity of the Holy Spirit demands, however, on the part of man himself that sort of free appropriation which is necessary in every personal act of a responsible moral agent and comes to its consummation in the co-working of those two factors in gradual progress.

Hollaz: "Ordinary illumination is not complete in one moment, but takes place through intervals of time by degrees, by acts frequently repeated, so that a man is disposed to admit a greater degree of light from time to time, yet so that if he repels the first grade of illumination, the Holy Spirit denies him the next and as long as that repulsion continues, because the second can have a place without the first.

"The proximate end of illumination is the regeneration and conversion of the sinner.

"The ultimate end of illumination is to be finally obtained in the kingdom of glory."

The Awakening.

The most direct operation of the calling and enlightening work is awakening. In our confession and in the old dogmaticians awakening is embraced in the very beginning, the *prima initia* of faith and conversion. The name awakening rests upon the divine call, "Awake thou that steepest, and arise from the dead," Eph. 5: 14. And a distinct element it was brought out more clearly and emphatically by the pietistic era of awakening under Spener, which was the awakening period in Germany; responding to the movements of Wesley and Whitefield in England and America. A peculiar abnormal illustration of it was the awakening of the children in Silesia in the eighteenth century and it is a marked feature of the popular religion of our own time-a great deal of labor and excitement beginning with the sinner before conversion and ending with awakening.

Martensen (Sec. 226) says: "Awakening precedes regeneration, but it does not constitute it. Awakening is certainly a work of grace, effecting the entire personality of the man, raising his consciousness to a high religious state...Grace kindles a new light in his soul (illumination); the kingdom of God rises within the man and he looks upon the world and upon himself in a new light...but although regeneration is certainly initiated thus, awakening is a state which precedes regeneration; but it is not yet the permanent indwelling (*inhabitatio*) of grace within the soul. The awakened man is as yet only roused by grace, he is not yet actually endowed with grace. There is still waiting the deciding resolve on his part, Awakening as such is only a state of religious distress and in the history of man's conversion, is the great point of crisis and of peril."

Thomasius says: "The pangs connected with the birth of the new man, the *prima initia*, in the case of many do not come to a decisive victory. In these stadia of beginning, much that is unsound and impure is wont to mix itself in. Especially is it common at this stage to build too much upon feelings and imaginations."

Difference Between Illumination and Regeneration.

Hollaz: "The former has respect more to the intellect, regeneration more to the will; the former consists formally of knowledge concerning sacred things from "the divine Word, the latter consists formally in the gift of faith. The effect of the former is the knowledge of the divine mysteries; the effect of the latter is confidence the merits of Christ. The former precedes, the latter follows."

Difference Between Illumination and Sanctification

Hollaz: "All Christians agree that sanctification, taken in a broader sense, embraces all the acts of applying grace; taken in a narrower sense, sanctification differs from illumination:

(1) "In regard to the particular subject, because in illumination the intellect is made more perfect, and in sanctification, the will;

(2) "In regard to the extent, because more are illuminated than sanctified;

(3) "In regard to their peculiar effect and design, because the effect of illumination is knowledge, or the supernatural knowledge of God and divine things, Eph. 18; 2 Cor. 4: 6, but the effect of sanctification is holiness and righteousness, Eph. 4: 24."

REGENERATION IN ITS NARROW SENSE.

The Scripture Doctrine.
Faith is the beginning of a new life in the power of the Holy Ghost. The divinely wrought entrance into this life is designated in Holy Scripture as a "being born again"; "born of the water and the Spirit." In it there is a "washing of regeneration and a renewing of the Holy Ghost."

Regeneration marks that act of God by which He produces in the inmost nature of man the beginning of a new life. It is called "newness of life," "newness of spirit"; he who receives it is called a new man and a new creature.

Usage of the Word Regeneration.
The word Regeneration is used in the Holy Scriptures, in our Confessions, and by our dogmaticians, in a two-fold sense-sometimes in a narrower sense, as designating the beginning of a new life, creating in man the power of exercising faith, sometimes in a more comprehensive or wider sense, as including justification and the renovation which follows it, and often it is used interchangeably.

Two-fold Usage in the New Testament.
The idea occurs in its stricter sense in the phrase "to be begotten of God," a favorite expression of St. John. Such faith from God is conceived by him as a single initial act, carrying in itself abiding issues. This is often expressed by the use of the perfect tense as in 1 John 1: 29; 4: 7; 5: 1, 4; John 3: 6, 8. In form and in context it is also implied in John 1: 12, 13. Just as clear is his language when he uses this thought in its meaning as regeneration in its wider sense as in John 20: 31; 1 John 2: 27, 29; 4:7. So likewise with St. Paul. The life in him was above all new; and it was of divine initiation or grace. Gal. 2: 20; 2 Cor. 5: 15-17. In Gal. 3: 11 it is taken for

remission of sins or justification and so in other passages. Paul uses the term with discrimination in its narrow sense in Tit. 3: 5.

Usage in Our Confessions.
In the Formula of Concord (Sol. Decl. III 19), reads, "The word regeneration is employed so as to comprise at the same time the forgiveness of sins alone for Christ's sake, and the succeeding renewal which the Holy Ghost works in those who are justified by faith." Again it is restricted to the remission of sins and adoption as sons of God and in this latter sense the word is much often used in the Apology, where it is written: "Justification is regeneration," although St. Paul has made a distinction between these words (Tit. 3: 5): "He saves us by the washing of regeneration and renewal of the Holy Ghost." As also the word vivification has sometimes been used in a like sense. For if a man is justified through faith (which the Holy Ghost alone works), this is truly a regeneration, because from a child of wrath he becomes a child of God, and thus is transferred from death, to life, as is written in Eph. 2: 5. Also: "The just shall live by faith" (Rom. 1: 17). In this sense the word is much and often used in the Apology.

> "Again it is often taken for sanctification and renewal which succeed the righteousness of faith, as Luther has thus used it in his book concerning the Church and the Councils, and elsewhere."

Usage by Our Dogmaticians.
In the Church doctrine as rendered at the Reformation, faith was brought into view in its two-fold character: as justifying us, it brought us into Christ as renewing us, it brought Christ into us.

In Luther's mode of apprehending the matter, justification precedes regeneration. In the dogmaticians since Calovius justification is put after regeneration. But there is no conflict in the thing itself. In Luther's case regeneration is taken in its more general sense as equivalent to the work of transitive conversion in which is involved the giving of faith. In the other regeneration is taken in its stricter sense. Regeneration strictly taken, and regeneration in its wider sense deduce diverse answers to the question which precedes justification.

If regeneration especially marks the beginning of the divine process it precedes justification; if it marks the consummation and thus by pre-eminence the end of the divine act, it follows justification in the order of thought. As the divine initial act it is first; as the divine final act it is last. When we look at regeneration as the beginning of the new life, we must say we are regenerated to faith.

When we look at regeneration in its wider sense including justification and sanctification, we must say we are regenerated by faith.

We here will discuss regeneration in its stricter sense as the beginning of the new life, and use it in sense of regeneration to faith.

The New Testament Teaching as to the Spiritual Nature of Man.
As a preface to our discussion we will quote the words of an eminent student of the Bible, "Besides the natural birthday the believer has a spiritual birthday in this life, and a birthday of glory in the life to come. The marks of regeneration are given in 1 John 3: 9, 14; 5:1.

Only if God's Spirit regenerate the spirit and soul will the same Spirit quicken to immortality and glory the body hereafter (Rom. 8: 11; Phil. 3: 21)."

The New Testament teaches more concerning the deeper things of the inner spiritual nature of man than those ever dream of, who are innocent of the exact usage of Greek words and of their exact exegesis by Greek scholars and careful commentators.

In the New Testament spirit (*pneuma*) denotes the distinctive self-consciousness, inner life of man, 1 Cor. 11; 5: 3; Col. 2: 5; Matt. 5: 3; Luke 1: 17; 1: 80, "wax strong in spirit"; 1 Cor. 5: 5; to the spirit the utterance of the will are referred, Acts 19: 21; Matt. 26: 41, "The spirit indeed is willing but the flesh is weak"; upon spirit all the affections of personal life operate, Acts 17:16; John 11: 33.

On this last verse Plummer remarks; *pneuma* is the seat of the religious emotions, the high innermost part of man's nature; the psyche (soul) is the seat of the natural affections and desires. Here and in John 13: 21 it is Christ's *pneuma* that is affected by the pressure of moral evil; in John 12: 27; Matt. 26: 38; Mark 14: 34, it is His psyche (soul), the seat of the natural emotions and affections, that is troubled, at the thought of impending suffering."

Cremer in his Biblico-Theological Lexicon of New Testament Greek says: "*Pneuma* often appears as parallel with *psyche* (soul) or *kardia* (heart), compare 1 Cor. 5: 3 with 1 Thess. 2: 17; John 13: 21 with 12: 27; John 14: 1, 27; etc., but between spirit and soul there is this important distinction, that the soul is represented as the subject of life, but the spirit never."

From many passages of Scripture, notably Luke 8: 55; James 2: 26; Gen. 2: 7; 6: 17; 7: 15, we must regard the spirit as the principle of life, which has an independent activity of its own in all the circumstances of perceptive and emotional life.

Death is described both as giving up of the *pneuma* and as a laying down or departure of the psyche; the former is said of Christ, Matt. 27: 50; Luke 23: 46; John 19: 30; of Stephen, Acts 7: 59, compare Luke 8: 55; the latter of Christ, John 10; 15, 17; Mark 10: 45 and elsewhere, John 12: 25; 13: 37, 38; Matt. 10: 39; yet there is a limit beyond which these expressions cannot be used interchangeably, but are clearly distinguished from each other, showing plainly that *pneuma* is the principle of life. So also there is a marked distinction between *pneuma* (spirit) and *kardia* (heart).

We may thus distinguish between the spirit principle, the soul subject, and the heart organ, of life.

Again, Cremer says: "The *pneuma* in man as the divine life principle, is at the same time the primitive of that God-regulated and therefore morally determined life which is peculiar to man (Gen. 1: 26, 27; Eph. 4: 24; 3: 10). Hence his *pneuma* is distinctively active or acted upon in all the relations of the religious, God-related life."

In Rom. 1: 9 we read, "God, whom I serve in my spirit," but in 2 Tim. 1; 3 we have, "God, whom I serve in a pure conscience, since a pure conscience is the result of the activity of the Spirit in the inner nature of man, that is, upon the spirit of man.

The *pneuma*, as the divine life principle and the principle of the divine God-related life, is spoken of in Rom. 8: 10, "If Christ is in you the body is dead because of sin, but the *pneuma* is life because of righteousness."

From Rom. 8: 16, "The Spirit Himself bears witness with our spirit that we are children of God." learn that the self-consciousness of the children of depends upon the contact of the

Spirit newly given them by God with the spirit in them which is theirs conformable with their nature.

From Rom. 8: 9, "But ye are not in the flesh but in the spirit, if it so be that the Spirit of God dwelleth in you. But if any man hath not the Spirit of Christ, he is none of His," we learn that the vitality and power of the divine life-principle depends upon the communication of the indwelling of the Spirit of Christ, for "as many as are indwelt by the Spirit of God these are sons of God...for ye received the spirit of adoption, whereby we cry, Abba Father" (Rom. 8: 14, 15).

Accordingly, we may say that by the communication of the Spirit (Gal. 3: 5) there is brought about a renewal of the human spirit or a revivification of the divine life principle. According to the context, we must understand by *pneuma* the divine life principle by nature peculiar to man, either in its natural condition, or as renewed by the communication of the Holy Spirit (Rom. 8: 10; 15: 23; Phil. 1: 27). In this renewal the *pneuma* is ever foremost as the active life-principle, Rom. 8: 4, 5, 6, 9.

This principle of the new life in man is described as "the spirit of adoption" Rom. 8: 15 (in contrast with "the spirit of bondage"), and the "spirit of faith" 2 Cor. 4: 13.

The *pneuma* forms the basis of the communion of the new creation (compare 2 Cor. 5: 17 with 1 Cor. 6:17); Phil. 1: 27, "that ye stand fast in one spirit"; Phil. 2: 1; Eph. 4: 3, 4.

The purpose and end of the work of the Holy Spirit upon the spirit of man is the strengthening of the inner man, Eph. 3: 16; 2 Cor. 6: 6; Gal. 3: 2, 5, 14.

Eph. 1: 13, "having heard the word of truth, having also believed, ye were sealed with the Holy Spirit of promise"; etc. Without entering upon a full discussion of the meaning of *nephesh* or psyche (soul) in the Old Testament, for which see Cremer, it will suffice to say that with Oehler and Delitzsch he holds that the soul is that personal life whose life principle is the *pneuma.*

In the New Testament psyche (soul) denotes life in the distinctness of individual existence and is used in a few places of living animals, Rev. 8: 9; 16; 3, "every living soul died." It is elsewhere used of man alone, primarily of the life belonging to the individual, Matt. 2: 20; Rom. 11: 3; Luke 12: 20; Acts 20: 10; etc.

Spirit and soul may be used synonymously in many cases and especially when the emotional life is referred to (compare

Matt. 11: 29 with 1 Cor. 16: 18; Acts 14: 22 with 1 Thess. 3: 13 (*kardias*); Luke 15: 46, 47, the expressions are not identical, for in Matt. 26: 38; 14: 34, "my soul is exceeding sorrowful, even unto death," it could hardly have been said, "my spirit is exceedingly sorrowful."

We find soul and spirit side by side in Heb. 4:12, "For the Word of God is living and active, and sharp than any two-edged sword and piercing even to the division of soul and spirit." Delitzsch in his Commentary says "*Pneuma* is the spirit in man, which carries in itself the divine image. This image, since the fall, has retired into itself, and so become for man as it were extinguishe4: At this point begin the operations of grace; man recall to mind his own true nature, though shadowed by sin[1] and that heavenly nature of man reappears when Christ is found in him. The Word of God, in discovering to a man the degree in which this precious gift has been lost or recovered, marks out and separates the *pneuma* in him.

"The psyche (soul), on the other hand, is a life emanating from the *pneuma*, when it is united with the body. The psyche has through sin become an unfree and licentious disharmony of energies and passions, and a powerless play-thing in the hands of material and demoniac influences. The Word of God exhibits to the man, the branch between the soul and the spirit, as penetrated by the Holy Spirit; and shows the abnormal monstrous condition of the soul controlled by the body...The divine Word is said to lay bare the whole man before the eyes of God and before the mind of man himself and discovers by means of a strict analysis both his psychico-spiritual and his inward corporeal condition."

In 1 Thess. 5: 23, "And the God of peace Himself sanctify you wholly (unhurt, in all its parts); and may your *pneuma* and psyche and *soma* be preserved entire." Cremer maintains correctly that *pneuma* is the divine life-principle (Rom. 8: 10); psyche, the individual life in which the *pneuma* is manifested; and soma the material organ vivified by the psyche. Thus the soul is the proper

---

[1] Delitzsch referring in a foot-note to the words of Luke 15: 17, "When he came to himself," said of the repentant. Prodigal, quotes with approval the words of Klee, "The fall of man was a two-fold process: first he fell out of God into himself then out of himself into nature. The process of his recovery likewise twofold: first he returns to himself in the consciousness of sin, and then with faith and repentance to God his Savior.

subject of life, whose salvation or preservation is the thing at stake in the presence of death, and accordingly we read, Acts 2: 27, "Thou wilt not leave my soul in Hades."

General Discussion.
The New Birth in the Light of Biblical Psychology.[2]
Before the fall, the spirit and soul of man were the exact image of God. Both were God's likeness, in their constitution and according to their life. Their background was the presence of God's love, by which they were maintained and preserved.

When man fell, spirit and soul did not cease to be God's likeness according to their constitution, for their substance remain unchanged; but they were so no longer according to their life, for in consequence of sin, the spirit, the life-principle of man, fell away from God, and the standing of peace and life with God was broken, and the effect was that the wrath of the holy justice of God was upon man.

Before the fall, the spirit and body of man were united by means of the soul to a self-living nature (a living soul, Gen. 2; 7), in which personality dwelt-to whose division it was left whether it would allow itself to be determined according to God's mind by the spirit in man the life-principle which immediately originated in God, would selfishly decide against God in its own separate life.

The spirit, instead of proving itself life-giving and an all-pervading power of life in ever increasing energy, fell under the bondage of the flesh and carnal emotions, in such a way, that, although its God-resembling substance continues still, its God-resembling life is quenched.

The soul of man instead of becoming spiritual, directed on all sides by the spirit that lives and moves in; God who was its source, became carnal and sensual. The spirit of the natural man is not what it was intended to be as the innermost nature of man-the personal might of the entire life. The soul, and the psychical in man has usurped the place of the spirit, and the spiritual.

For our salvation, in Christ a new beginning is established. The Logos united Himself inseparably to human nature in its three-fold human life, of spirit, soul, and body, but differed from

---

[2] In this discussion, we are much indebted to Delitzsch, Biblical Psychology, 381, 401.

fallen man in that He was without sin, and the Apostle Paul says His *pneuma* was a life-giving spirit (1 Cor. 15: 45).

As we all have Adam's nature by birth, so we must be created anew and become partakers of Christ's nature, if we wish to enter into the heavenly kingdom. The Logos assumed a human nature and because a true human nature was united to the Logos, Christ is a life-giving spirit to man, and as God dwelt in Him bodily, the Spirit of Christ can give spiritual life to man.

"As we have borne the image of the earthy, we must also bear the image of the heavenly" (1 Cor. 15: 49), that is, we must become inwardly like to Christ, by being translated from the position of being ruled by a carnal and sensual soul, into the position of being ruled by a life-giving spirit; for without participation in the life-giving spirit of the incarnate One we have no part in the spiritual body of the Risen and Exalted One.

We have a share in the body, soul, and spirit of the first Adam, by means of physical begetting. A new humanity could not possibly originate from Christ in this manner. It originates by means of a new creation, which moreover is a birth, but as a birth from above, it is essentially different from the earthly or natural birth.

The new creation finds the ungodly being of man in existence, and transforms it into a godly one. Its point of entrance into the inmost nature of man, his spirit, is in his conscience which. is the remains of the image of God in man. This work of creation is completed by changing the godlessness of man, his separation from God into fellowship with God, for the preaching of the Word in the adult and unbaptized man through the Holy Spirit begins a new life in man, and through the Law condemns sin and convicts man of sin, and through the Gospel promises forgiveness of sins, and if the man does not reject the Word of God, grants the supernatural power to lay hold of the promises of the Word and receive the Spirit through which the faith is enkindled.

This Word of God then leads also to baptism, in which, faith is increased, the forgiveness made sure, and the believer sealed and implanted into Christ's life, for in baptism he puts on Christ.

This internal operation which addresses itself to the innermost nature of man, to the spirit of the mind is unalterably referred to God, and changes the relation of man to God, and makes his conscience into a good one and bestows faith and forgiveness of sins, even justification, and thus the work of grace begins. Its first operation is free love and grace on God's side to meet man; on man's side a change of consciousness brought about by the power of God and God works the power that man receives the grace and exercises faith, for it is all of grace and faith alone.

The transference of the human ego out of the principle of wrath into the principle of love and faith makes the beginning of the new life, and marks the regeneration in its narrow sense.

Other divine agencies are added to this one of the regeneration of man's spirit, by which sinful man is made a partaker of the spirit, the soul, and the body of Christ. There proceed from Christ according to Him a three-fold human condition certain agencies which establish man, in the way of participation with Christ's spirit, soul, and body, in a fellowship which is powerful to transform man's own spirit, his own soul, and his own body.

(1) We receive of the spirit of Christ, which: after Christ's resurrection is combined into one with the Holy Spirit, as is shown by the Pentecostal gift. This communication of the Spirit revives the extinguished image of God in our spirit, and keeps it living, and, restores our spirit to its true nature, so that for the first time again our spirit becomes spiritual (1 Cor. 2: 12-16); The work of grace consists precisely in this, that it realizes again the lost god-like nature of the spirit, that is called again to rule the soul, and develops a spiritual beginning of the man thus once again restored (1 Cor. 15: 45).

(2) We receive of Christ's soul, for we receive of Christ's blood in the sacrament of the Lord's Supper, for the soul is in the blood (Lev. 17; 11). Delitzsch remarks: "This divine-human blood of the Mediator, now Exalted, becomes the tincture of our soul...and by virtue of this blood, and of the spirit which in Christ's spirit has again become God's, the soul recovers its god- like glory, if not at once in mid-day clearness yet still as it were, in morning twilight and dawning."

In the essential relation in which soul stands to the body, this is also to the advantage of the body—but we receive, moreover,

(3) Of the flesh of Christ, which is pervaded by the life-giving Spirit, and is of the nature of spirit and is communicable for spiritual benefit, "for the words that I have spoken unto you are spirit and are life" (John 6: 63).

Delitzsch says: "This flesh which He Himself calls heavenly bread of life, and manna that makes immortal, enters into us without mingling with sin—pervaded materialistic flesh...and becomes an assurance and pledge of life in the midst of death, a tincture of immortality."

These three divine agencies peculiar to the New Testament, proceeding from Christ's spirit, soul, and body upon our spirit, soul, and body (1 Thess. 5: 23), may be called the regeneration of the natural life.

In what distinct way the means of grace, the Word and the Sacraments, serve in increasing the power of regeneration (in its wider sense) in the new man according to the likeness of Christ, will be discussed in its proper place.

The Unconscious and Conscious Side of Grace in this Regeneration of the Adult.[3]

John 3: 7, 8, "Marvel not that I said unto thee, ye must be born anew. The wind bloweth where it listeth, and thou hearest the voice thereof, but knowest not whence it cometh and whither it goeth: so is every one that is born of the spirit."

Jesus, desirous of explaining that the birth from above is not sensible and natural, in condescension to Nicodemus makes use of a parable drawn from the region of nature. As the wind bloweth where it listeth, now here, now there, without being subject to limits and without allowing its paths to be described, and as we cannot determine where it first began, and how far at the time it may go, or where it may cease; so it is with everyone that is born of the Spirit.

The operation of the Spirit of regeneration is therefore,

(1) A free one, withdrawn from the power of human volition, of human special agency;

(2) A mysterious one, lying beyond human consciousness, and only to be recognized by its effects.

The regenerated person recognizes himself as a man, with a fundamentally changed tendency in all his powers, released by the sprinkling with Christ's blood, from his previously evil conscience, instead of a child of wrath being once more a child o!

---

[3] Compare Delitzsch, Biblical Psychology, pp. 401-404.

God, renewed in the foundations of his nature according to the image of God, and justified by the grace of redemption.

He hears the voice of the Spirit, he recognizes the discipline of the Holy Spirit manifesting itself in many ways, in instruction, warning, reproof; he knows himself: as in the actual possession of the Holy Spirit but all these things he knows only as the results of that which has taken place in him.

As in the natural birth, so in the spiritual birth; the basis and beginning of his spiritual conscious life remains hidden from him in darkness. He is conscious of that which is affected, but only as the result of a spiritual work that has taken place in the region of his unconsciousness.

The creature which God establishes into actual existence is absolutely passive in regeneration. Even the first operation of grace which overpowers us occurs in us. as in the condition of sleep in death, Eph. 5: 14, "Awake, thou that sleepest and arise from the dead, and Christ shall shine upon thee." And while the faith Which the grace of God affects is a fact of our consciousness, yet the events themselves, named and promised by the Word, all occur in us in the depth of unconscious and only now and then reflections of them fall from upon our consciousness.

The God-man communicates to us His essential fullness, and makes us partakers of His nature, and at the time partakers of the divine nature (2 Pet. 1: 4), in Triune God who is internally present to us, and surrounds and pervades us, but we are able neither to contemplate, nor even to distinguish, these divine agencies in beginning and progress.

We know from the Word and from the testimony of the Spirit by means of the Word, what is bestowed upon us by grace (1 Cor. 2: 12); but we know it is in faith.

It is therefore clear that the fact of our regeneration in its narrow sense takes place in the region of our unconsciousness.

The Unconscious Side of Grace in the Regeneration of the Infant.[4]
In our discussion we have not yet at all referred to infant baptism as a means of regeneration, as we have treated of the unbaptized adult regenerated by the preaching of the Word, which leads and points to baptism as the means by which man is sealed, the

---

[4] Compare Delitzsch, Biblical Psychology, pp. 405-407.

forgiveness of sins bestowed, and by which he is engrafted into Christ.

The sacrament of holy baptism may prove even in the newly born child to be the means of regeneration, and the Holy Spirit may operate on the natural life of the child and make the beginning of a spiritual life; especially as the adult can do nothing positively in his regeneration, but can only do something negatively, can only resist God's grace and reject the working of God's Spirit.

On the part of the infant there is no resistance and it is easier for the child to be born in the kingdom of God than for an adult sinner whose will has first to be overcome, and no one can be born again, unless you become as a child, "for of such is the kingdom of heaven" Matt. 19: 14; Mark 10: 14; Luke 18: 16.

There is nothing on the part of the child to prevent its regeneration and God has the power and everyone having the nature of man must be born again in order to become a member of the kingdom of heaven.

But all regenerate life has faith as its indispensable postulate. The whole subject whether we should baptize infants concentrates itself in the minds of our dogmaticians in the question whether infants are able to believe, and what kind of faith, it can be said that they have. They all recognize the conclusion that he who is not capable of faith (*capax fidei*) is, moreover, not capable of regeneration (*capax regenerationis*). And this conclusion is perfectly scriptural.

If it be supposed that, in the child that is to be baptized, the necessity for redemption and the desire for redemption takes the place of faith, the enigma is not solved. If by baptism the child is only transferred with the possibility of regeneration to be realized subsequently (which is confessedly the prevalent view of the Reformed Churches), then baptism, which finds in the child no obstacle of opposition as in the unbelieving adult is emptied of the peculiar efficiency attested by Scripture.

The view so often expressed since the time of Augustine, that the want of faith and intention on the part of the child may be supplied by the faith of the sponsors and of the whole Church, needs no refutation. The justification of infant baptism remains without evasion conditioned by the question whether infants can believe.

If faith were a work of man's own, with the human initiation, always conscious and discursive or reflective, then this question would have to be answered absolutely in the negative.

But if faith may also be a human condition of divine operation, a work of grace that changes man's inner relation to God, there is left a possibility to reply to this question in the affirmative.

Brenz draws a distinction between a hidden (*abscondita*) and a manifest (*revelata*) faith, ascribing the first to children, while others distinguish between immediate and mediate faith, and Hollaz says: "Infants have faith, not reflective or discursive, but direct and simple."

As we wish to enter more fully upon the discussion of the question, it is of the greatest importance for the right judgment of the spiritual life to choose the most appropriate designation, and thus we maintain that on the part of the child faith is direct and not conscious, or discursive, which latter belongs to adult life.

The Faith of an Infant is Direct, not Conscious or Discursive Like That of an Adult.

In baptism the Spirit is offered to the child which does not resist its working, but the Spirit creates in the child the power to receive the grace of God and imparts to it the spiritual life and engrafts the child into Christ. The presence of the Holy Spirit purifies and, cleanses and bestows through regeneration the beginning of the new life and justifies and sanctifies the conscience of the child and the child receives the gift of God because it does not resist that which is given, and thus is born into the kingdom of God. This non-resistance on the part of the child, this power to receive the gift of regeneration and justification, which is the work of God, we call direct faith instead of conscious or discursive faith on the part of the adult.

We meet with this distinction between direct and conscious or discursive faith in other parts of the New Testament.

In that famous first chapter of Romans (1: 20, 21), Paul says that the heathen "though knowing God," glorified Him not as God, and in 1 Thess. 4: 5; Gal. 4: 8, he describes them as "not knowing God." There is no conflict here. The meaning of the apostle doubtless is that God reveals Himself to all men by His works; they have an organ of perception corresponding to His revelation in nature; they all really acknowledge Him as God by direct act, what Tholuck calls a "potent latent knowledge" but their knowledge has never come to inner assent to this self-revelation of God, never to an internal comprehension of God. Men did not regard it as worth the trouble to have God in their knowledge. Their ungodly will did not permit the result to be produced which they spiritually perceived by a direct act.

So likewise in the prologue of St. John's Gospel. In John 1: 4, when the apostle says "and the life was the light of men," he regards this statement wholly apart from the relation of men to that life, for in 1: 5 he is constrained to complain that the light which shone in darkness was not welcomed by many to be enlightened by the true light beams without exception upon man: it has the destination, and the power, and the desire to enlighten every man; but the world of humanity acknowledge Him. The direct act is divine, not human. A divine power offers but man stifles the growth of the recognition at the moment when it ought to begin.

So it is with the means of grace, the Word and Sacrament. Even although the adult purposely restrains all wholesome reflection upon the Word, once understood still the Word bas a power directly proceeding from it, an ideal objectivity. He bears it in his knowledge and memory, "although the word of hearing him, because it is not united with faith" (Heb. 4: 2). It is in him as a seed fallen upon ground-for the man is as dead and is asleep-but sell the Word is living and so soon as the ground or human heart becomes loosened, strikes root and shoots forth. As long as the man resists the Word in him, it is as a power of judgment. But in the very fact that he knows the Word of the Grace of God in Christ, he has great advantage over him that knows it not; for he need only to forsake his resistance, and the Word in him will manifest itself as a power for the enlightenment of hl spirit and the changing of his personal life. What is true of the Word in the event of attaining to man's knowledge is true also of the Sacrament of baptism. The condition of its saving reception is faith, whether direct as on the part of the child, or conscious and discursive as in the case of the adult.

He who is baptized, even if he has not received baptism in a conscious mental comprehension, needs not to be baptized again. The substantial contents of the sacrament have attained in him a living presence once for all, and there needs only a conscious faith, that it may realize itself in a reflex manner in himself to his salvation which he already has inwardly present by direct act, and which ever presses to be realized in him.

The substantial completeness of the sacrament of baptism is in no case dependent on the faith of the believer.

The sacraments as means of grace are brought into immediate nearness to man. They are given to man by God for the purpose that he should appropriate them to himself by means of faith.

God is Spirit, and makes Himself present in man as, and by what means, He will. He can encircle man with His wrath, or in grace with His love. By the sacrament of baptism He makes Himself present to man in the whole light of His redeeming, regenerating love. Much is conferred upon man by the grace of baptism—a treasure is concealed in his field-he can uncover it at any time.[5]

The direct results of the grace of God, in baptism, going forth on the child, and surrounding it, is the direct act of direct faith; a power to receive the gift of God, a communion with Christ, a creation of a spiritual nature in Christ, justification even the forgiveness of sins.

This direct act has in itself the promise of God. The conscious act of faith, in the case of the adult of divine assurance, of joyous self-certainty, of experience, Seeing and tasting, belong not to the essence of justifying faith; but the former, the direct faith, is as our older dogmaticians say, the form of essential faith.

Pontoppidan (d. 1764) says: "It is necessary acknowledge a two-fold manifestation of faith. The called *actio directa*, by which we lay hold of and embrace Christ; the other *actio reflexa*, by which we acknowledge our own doing, and feel or experience that we apprehended Christ. By the former we believe, to speak accurately, on Christ; by the second, however, we become assured of the fact that we believe and the faith has laid hold on Christ falls back softly and sweet into itself. But there are many who have really laid on Christ, although they do not feel that they have Him; and these are none the less justified. We become incontestably righteous by the *actio directa* and not by the *actio reflexa*: we

---

[5] Thomasius already uses this number.

become justified, not because we feel that we believe, but so far as we only believe."

And Delitzsch says: "The faith is thus in its essence *fiducia supplex* (assurance of refuge), not *fiducia triumphans seu gloriosa* (assurance of experience).

If faith as a direct act, be the work of God, which must be introduced into the adult through the Word and baptism, why cannot the grace of regeneration effect even in the child the direct faith is necessary to its saving reception. It is said that faith is not possible, and not conceivable, without consciousness, but the condition of the child is certainly not the absolute opposite of consciousness. The natural life in its true essence, although in its first beginning of development, is present immediately and is already a growing consciousness. The child, from the very beginning, is an entire man, growing on all sides, and is a person. Why should God not be able to effect in the remotely glimmering consciousness of the child a germinal faith, just as well as a developed faith in the consciousness of the adult?

Faith in its maturer condition certainly subsists in the perfectly Conscious acts of apprehension *cognoscitiva* (knowledge), *approbativa* (assent) and *appropriativa* (confidence), but every believer knows from experience, that true faith began with a secret divine agent upon his will and that this develops these acts of faith. Why should God not be able to begin His agency upon the conscience and inner spiritual life of the child? Such an inclination to Christ, effected by God, is possible in little children (Matt. 18: 6), "These little ones which believe on me" and is not impossible to newly born children, for the natural consciousness begins from a remote point of growth and this direct faith must be able to begin from a remote point of growth, and may be present in seed and germ from the very time of baptism.

We are teaching nothing new, for our older dogmaticians teach the same, and so do our modern, and we need only refer to Thomasius and Martensen. It has always been the testimony of the Church and her teachers, that there are operations of divine grace which stimulate or move the will and precede self-consciousness.

The Church Doctrine.
Teaching of our Dogmaticians.

Definition of Regeneration.
Baier: "Regeneration is an action of God, by which he endows man destitute of spiritual strength, but obstinately resisting, out of His mere grace for Christ's sake, by means of the Word and baptism, on the part of the intellect and the will, with spiritual powers to in Christ, and thus to commence a spiritual life in order that he may attain justification, renovation, and eternal salvation."

The Point From Which it Proceeds is the Death of Sin.
Quenstedt: "In particular, on the side of intellect the starting point is great blindness and uniform debility in regard to the saving knowledge of Eph. 5: 8; John 1: 5; 1 Cor. 2: 14. On the part will the like incapacity of embracing savingly the good offered in the Gospel, Rom. 8: 7."

Its Goal is a Spiritual Life.
Quenstedt: "In particular on the part of the intellect, it is both a spiritual capacity of the mind savingly to know the object which brings salvation, 2 Cor. 4:6, and then an actual saving knowledge of it; on the Part of the will, a confident reclining of the heart on the known good, Rom. 6: 11."

Distinction Between Regeneration of Adults and Children.
Hollaz: "We discuss now principally the regeneration of the intellect and will of adult sinners; regeneration of the intellect of children is somewhat more difficult of comprehension. But we do not doubt that the intellect of infants in regeneration is imbued with a saving knowledge of God by the Holy Spirit in baptism, and their will is endowed with confidence in Christ. We agree here with the views of Chemnitz."

Chemnitz: "When we say that infants believe or have faith, it is not meant that they understand or have consciousness of faith, but the error is rejected that baptized infants are pleasing to God, and are saved without any action of the Holy Spirit in them. This is certain, that the Holy Spirit is efficacious in them, so that they can receive the grace of God and the remission of sins. The Holy Spirit operates in them in His own which it is not in our power to explain. That operation of the Spirit in infants we call faith, and we affirm that they believe. For that mean, or organ, by which the kingdom of God, offered in the Word and Sacraments, is received, the Scripture calls faith, and declares that believers receive the kingdom of God. And Christ affirmed in Mark 10: 15, that adults receive the kingdom of God the same way that a little child receives it; and, M 18: 6. He speaks of the little ones which believe in Him."

Krauth: "By nature the infant is as really a sinner, and by grace as really a believer as the adult is, though it can neither do sin nor exercise faith. It has sin by nature, and has faith by grace. Working out under the law of the first condition it will inevitably do sin, as under the law of the second it will exercise faith. Faith justifies by its receptivity alone. There is no justifying merit in faith as an act, nor is there any in the acts it originates. In the adult it is divinely wrought: it is 'not of ourselves, it is the gift of God.' In the infant there is wrought by God through the Holy Ghost, by means of the water and the Word, that condition of receptivity which it has not by nature. The Holy Ghost offers grace, and so changes the moral nature of the child that this nature becomes receptive of the grace offered. This divinely wrought condition we call receptive faith, and though its phenomena are suspended, it is really faith, and as really what is essential to justification, as does the faith of the adult. The hand of an infant may as really a diamond as if the infant knew the value of the treasure it held, and if the natural hand can be the minister of acts whose force it comprehends not, how much more may the supernatural hand."

The Form of Regeneration.
Hollaz: "The form of regeneration is in the of spiritual life; that is, in the bestowment of the power of believing, and of saving faith; or, in the illumination of our mind, and the production of confidence in our heart or as it is otherwise expressed, in the gift itself of faith.

This Spiritual Change is not a Substantial One.
Quenstedt: "In regeneration, the same natural substance of our bodies remains, the properties only being changed. Regeneration does not destroy nature but perfects and directs it; it does not change it so it ceases to be nature."

Regeneration is a New Creation.
Quenstedt: "The regenerated man is 'a new man' and 'a new creature', 2 Cor. 5: 17; Gal. 6: 15, on account of the new spiritual

strength imparted in regeneration and renovation, by which the image of God is repaired, consisting in the knowledge of God, Col. 3: 10; in righteousness and true holiness, Eph. 4: 24."

The Regeneration of Infants is Instantaneous.

Hollaz: "In infants, as there is not an earnest and obstinate resistance, the grace of the Holy Spirit accompanying baptism breaks and restrains their natural resistance that it may not impede regeneration; wherefore, their regeneration takes place instantaneously."

The Ordinary Regeneration of Adults is Successive.

Hollaz: "In the regeneration of adults there are many difficulties to be removed by care, and illumination and instruction extended over a long time are to be afforded from the divine Word, until a full faith is kindled in the mind."

Regeneration on the Part of God is Perfect.

Quenstedt: "Regeneration on the part of God regenerating is perfect, and so does not admit of a greater and less degree any more than carnal generation." Here regeneration is used in the narrow sense.

On the Part of Men Receiving it is Imperfect.

Quenstedt: "Because sinners imperfectly receive the influence of the Holy Spirit, because moral evil is always near them, Rom. 7: 23; because sin still dwells in them, Rom. 7: 17, 18; and because faith can grow and increase in them." Here regeneration is used in the broader sense.

Regeneration can be Resisted.

Hollaz: "Regeneration is the action of the Holy Spirit efficacious and sufficient to produce faith but it can be resisted (Acts 18: 5, 6)."

Quenstedt: "The regenerating grace of God is always efficacious in itself, although it does not always proceed to the second act, on account of the resistance of the subject to be regenerated. Its efficacy is limited and exerting itself through the mediation of the Word and Sacraments."

Regeneration in the Broad Sense may be Lost.

"The grace of regeneration is lost sins subversive of conscience are deliberately committed (1 Tim. 1: 19). But regeneration lost may be recovered by the penitent (Gal. 4: 19)."

Regeneration in the Narrow Sense Always Remains Alive.
Schmid: "The way of return to the God, so long as life lasts, is open to him who has from grace."

Difference Between Regeneration and Conversion.
Our dogmaticians ordinarily give this difference: "The two differ 1) in regard to the subjects; regeneration pertains to adults and children; conversion properly to adults, as children cannot properly be said to be converted; 2) in regard to the means, regeneration is effected by the Word and Sacraments; conversion the Word alone."

V. CONVERSION.

Even in the natural state of man's life he experiences manifold moral operations of the Spirit of God. But not until he experiences the renewing efficacy of the Holy Spirit's grace in the eternal life of his will, is he placed in the position in which he can turn and determine to turn away from sin and to God.

This turning from, and turning to, is subjective conversion. This conversion, the internal process essential to the salvation of every man, is therefore grounded alone in the operation of grace, and by grace alone made possible: yet in the act itself as consummated, there is the internal decision of the will of man. He converts or turns, because he is converted or turned. What he does is conditioned by what is done in him: and this is done in him in order that he may do what God demands. He is not, even his conversion, a passive piece of mechanism, but a truly moral agent. He is not turned as matter or as an animal, but he is turned as a man, that is, he is converted.

The Uses of the Word Conversion.
The word is used in a four-fold sense:

1) It is used in the widest sense, as indicating not transfer from a state of sin, but as including justification, regeneration in the broad sense, renovation and preservation in peace.

So sometimes in the Apology and Formula of Concord, and by some of our older dogmaticians. This is often the usage in a popular sense when we say, he is a converted man, that is, a true Christian, justified, regenerated (in the broad sense), a child of God,

2) It is used in a wide sense as involving repentance and faith, as we say, the man leads a life of conversion, including repentance and faith, and he must continue thus through life.

3) It is used in a stricter sense, so used also Scripture, inasmuch at one-time God is said to convert man, and at another time, man is urged to convert himself; referring both to the same action.

In this sense it is called transitive conversion, because the act of God who is the agent does not terminate in God, but passes over into man and the act of man thus receiving and carrying out the operation of God, is called intransitive conversion. God is active (regenerating grace) as far as it proceeds from God, and man is passive in so far as it is received by man.

4) It is used in the most strict sense as intransitive conversion or the repentance by which the sinner is said to convert himself by means of the strength imparted by regenerating and converting grace. In this sense we here use the word.

The Scripture Doctrine.

The Holy Scriptures designate conversion partly as a work of grace and partly as something required of man. The noun "conversion" (*epistrophe*) occurs only once in the Authorized Version in Acts 15: 3 declaring the conversion of the Gentiles.

The verb "to convert" (*epistrepho*), from which the noun is formed, is used frequently in the sense (1) of a physical turning about, but (2) most frequently of a turning about from sin to God, a returning from the paths of sin to the path of life. Sometimes it is translated in the passive sense, in the Authorized Version as in Matt. 13: 15; Luke 22: 32; Acts 3: 19, but not so in the Revised Version. It is generally active, sometimes transitive as in Luke 1: 16, 17; James 5: 19, 20. But most generally intransitive as in Matt. 13: 15; Luke 22: 32; Acts 9: 35; 11: 21; 14: 15; 2 Cor. 3: 16, etc. The negative and positive elements are completely blended in Acts 14: 15; 1 Thess. 1: 9; Acts 26: 18. The negative element implied in the word is often left out and only the positive sense retained as in Acts 9: 35; 2 Cor. 3: 16; Acts 26: 20; 1 Pet. 2: 25. The verb frequently means to change and convert oneself as in Matt. 13: 15; Mark 4: 12; John 12: 40, etc. Sometimes it includes to believe as in Acts 11: 21 and 9:35. As it is a turning from a certain state or conduct so it signifies a positive entrance upon a certain state or conduct, namely, into fellowship with and possession of salvation, out of a state of remoteness and lack of grace. it differs from to repent, which includes only the behavior as the turning of penitence. Conversion combines penitence and faith, Acts 20: 21.

It is often represented as the divine work, not infrequently is referred to the instrumental cause, the human minister, James 5: 19, 20.

According, then, to the nature of the case, conversion is referred to God as the absolute cause, to the servant or minister of God as the instrumental cause, to man as the moral agent acted upon and enabled to turn.

The word *strepho* is used but once in the *Textus Receptus* for conversion (Matt. 18: 3), but the modern critical editors add John 12:40.

The Church Doctrine.
Usage of the Old Dogmaticians.
As regards the mere use of terms our old divines differ somewhat from the present practice. The old dogmaticians, as for example, Koenig and Quenstedt, treat first of regeneration, then of conversion, yet in such a way that both the conceptions concur in the main in essential respects and differ more in form than in substance.

Regeneration in the broader sense is the renewing of the spiritual life in general, involving justification and the renovation which follows it, using the word in the widest sense as we have outlined.

In the narrower sense they use it either as identical with the forgiveness of sin or justification; or, taken in the stricter dogmatic sense, it is the imparting of the power of believing. It may be taken either upon the one side as active and transitive; or on the other as passive.

Regeneration in the active, transitive sense, designates the operation of God which imparts to man the new spiritual life, and this is the ordinary dogmatic sense of regeneration. Passively it designates the spiritual change in the man himself.

In the same way conversion taken in the broader sense means the entire placing of the man in the condition of faith involving justification and renovation.

Strictly taken, however, and this is the proper dogmatic sense of the word, it is distinguished from justification and renovation, and is either active and transitive, or is passive.

Active and transitive, it marks the converting efficacy of the Holy Spirit, turning man from unbelief to faith.

Passively, it marks the internal spiritual change in the mind and will of man himself.

Hollaz adds to the active and passive sense of conversion, the intransitive, by which he designates the immanent and reciprocal act of the will by which the sinner is said to convert himself, Acts 3: 19. He converts himself not by powers native to him, not innate in him, but given to him.

The Freedom of Man.

The problem of the doctrine of conversion involves in relation to the divine operation of grace the freedom of man. (See Anthropology pp. 147-178.)

There comes in here a double element to be considered: (1) the preparation for conversion in the life of one not yet regenerated; and (2) the relation of the Will to grace in conversion itself. In regard to the former it is acknowledged that it is for the unregenerate man to submit himself externally to the means of grace.

Whatever may be the bondage of the will under it does not prevent a man from exercising his natural freedom in reading the Bible, in hearing sermons, in conversation with Christians; nor in general, does it prevent acts of a purely external nature with regard to the means of grace, and if the means of grace, in their very nature as a constant organ of the Holy Spirit place a man of the absolute helplessness of mere nature, the problem of personal responsibilities does not seem difficult solve. By what man can do by nature, he may come where these means of grace are found, within that circle where all is done efficiently by God.

In regard to the relation of the will to grace in conversion all that is positive is to be referred to God; whilst it is His work, He respects even in their abuse, the sanity of personal freedom and responsibility.

We cannot be converted by our will, nor by powers of reason, nor by all the natural processes which our natural powers are developed. Neither can we be converted against our will, and form a new life in our will. In the period immediately following conversion are co-workers with God. There is no synergism before conversion, but after conversion all is synergism, the conjoined working of the renewed will with the will of God.

Difference Between Regeneration and Conversion.

Thus there remains between regeneration and conversion only the formal difference that regeneration takes place also with children and can be wrought through the sacrament of baptism, while conversion takes place with adults—those who have ceased to be infants-and is wrought through the Word as well as through the Sacraments. It has been said that in this mode of conceiving and defining conversion there is lacking the element of the moral personal activity of man and that consequently, there is a defect in the dogmatic conception of the doctrine, and that the distinction between conversion and the divine act of regeneration is darkened. Hollaz adds to the active and passive conception of conversion the intransitive as Baier had done before him, according to which, it signifies an immanent and reciprocal act of will by which the sinner is said to convert himself, as in Acts 3: 19, "repent ye therefore, and turn again," the verb is in the first aorist imperative active and the Revised Version is the correct translation.

The transitive conversion, the work that God does, is identical with regeneration. With Hollaz intransitive conversion is the terminus and effect of transitive conversion, and is that repentance in which the sinner, through the powers conferred upon him by converting grace and passively received, is said to convert himself, wherefore the sinner converts himself not by powers native to him, but by powers given to him.

This conception of intransitive conversion involves the relation of the working of divine grace to the attribute of man as a free moral agent. The development of the church doctrine on this point belongs essentially to the discussion of Free Will, which see in my treatment on Anthropology.

Preparation for Conversion.
There comes in here a double element to be considered, (1) the preparation for conversion in the life of one not yet regenerate; and (2) the relation of the will to grace in conversion itself.

As regards preparation, the antecedent process of conversion in the life of the unregenerate, the Formula of Concord simply refers to the possibility of using the means of grace.

Aegidius Hunnius, in his work on *Providence of God and Predestination* (1595) and on *Free Will* (1597), attributes to the natural man desire of learning and knowing in reference to the truth of salvation; especially appealing to Amos 8; 11, which speaks of God sending a famine and thirst of hearing the Word of God and o wandering and running to and fro to seek the Word of the Lord. Musaeus has handled this question most thoroughly in his *Disputations* (1647-49), and in his *Theological Tractates concerning Conversion* (1661).

He ascribes to the natural man in reference to spiritual things certain pedagogic acts of knowledge and will which can proceed so as to produce a certain general pleasure in the idea of salvation, a simple complacency, without however implying that conversion is therewith actually begun, or that these are properly spiritual acts, connected with the pious desire or with the effort least tending to those good things as things to be required.

This mode or statement, however, produced a decided contradiction on the part of the Wittenberg divine. Yet more was this the case, especially in the person Calovius, with reference to the mode of teaching adopted by the Helmstedt divines. Some of these placed between spiritual actions and civil works the additional department of moral works, for which they demanded a divine grace in the general sense.

Only the more strictly did the most of the others, the orthodox dogmaticians, oppose the inferior and the superior hemispheres to one another, and referred to the inferior hemispheres only the acts of external religion, so that every desire of information from the Word or desire of eternal salvation already involves a work of prevenient applying grace, and thus no more is left to the natural man than a desire, not so much after truth as alter novelty, a desire of knowing divine things after the manner common to any other sort of knowledge.

A change in some respects, however in the mode of stating the doctrine was precluded by the development of the doctrine of general and indirect Vocation by which was brought out the idea of prevenient grace, outside of the sphere of applying grace, and by this prevenient grace were wrought the pedagogic acts. Buddaeus especially gave an impulse to this phase of doctrine. The principle concerning prevenient grace, in the general sense, became naturalized especially in connection with the experiences derived from the work of heathen missions, and extended itself more and more in the Church. During the period of Illumination and Rationalism the natural powers were exalted at the cost of the necessity of grace.

Theology of the More Recent Period.

The theology of the recent period has again renewed the church doctrine of grace, emphasizing however with more or less force, the principle which Julius Mueller has expressed with these words: "That man before his conversion and before the operation of divine grace within him, must be capable of a drawing and a longing towards these eternal blessings which the word of God offers." This proposition is true in one sense. Man is Certainly capable of being drawn, but is not capable of going without the drawing. If the capacity claimed involves a self-produced fitness wrought apart from grace the proposition is not true. With this, therefore, is connected another question, whether man by this natural drawing to what is higher has the power of appropriating for himself saving grace. To affirm this is to affirm in substance the old synergistic view.

And this is virtually the view of Julius Mueller, Delitzsch, and Martensen. Or it is asked whether that natural drawing is only the starting point for the operation of saving grace, which grace alone makes it actually possible for man to overcome the natural aversion to grace and lay hold of it.

This latter is the true view, and has been defended among others of recent date by Thomasius.

The Relation of the Will to Grace.

As regards the relation of the will to grace in conversion the orthodox dogmatics follows in general the Formula of Concord.

The article has laid stress upon the divine factor in conversion, dwelling upon the transitive conversion; The Formula of Concord does not allow of any proper activity of our own will in divine things before conversion, in conversion and when conversion is taken transitively. This is indubitably true.

The conversion which God works, He works alone. No transitive act but His occurs in conversion. The Formula of Concord says (569): "Man's will is purely passive" that is, "Man of himself, or from his natural powers, cannot contribute anything or help to his conversion, and that conversion is not only in part, but altogether an operation, gift and present and work of the Holy Ghost alone, who accomplishes and affects it, by His virtue and power, through the Word, the understanding, will and heart of man, where man does or works nothing, but only suffers." It likewise says (499, 17): "It is correctly said that, in conversion, God, through the drawing of the Holy Ghost, changes stubborn and unwilling into willing men, and that such conversion, in the daily exercise of repentance, the regenerate will of man is not idle, but also cooperates with all the deeds of the Holy Ghost which He works through us."

It may clear up the difficulty sometimes felt in connection with the strong phraseology of the Formula of Concord and of our old theologians in regard to the passiveness of man to remember that the point they wish to secure is that the first decisive saving movement, the *sine qua non* of any second one, comes from God and not from man. It is not man's activity but man's receptivity, man's passive capacity or passivity which alone can be affected by this.

The whole question in a few words is: Who begins the saving work? Does man begin it? To say he does, this is Pelagianism. Or do both God and man begin it? To say so—this is Synergism. Or does God alone begin it? This is the Scripture doctrine, and this is the vital point of our old divines.

Chemnitz, in his Loci, says: "Conversion is not a change which is finished and perfected in all its parts in one moment, but it has its beginnings and its progress in which, at length, it is perfected in great infirmity. No, man, therefore, may think: I may wait with an evil and idle will, until my renewal or conversion is accomplished by the Holy Spirit without any movement on .my part. For it cannot be shown at what mathematical point the liberated will begins to act, but when prevenient grace, that is, when the first beginnings of faith and conversion, are given to man, the wrestling of the flesh and spirit at once begins. And it is manifest that the wrestling is not made without a movement of our will. After the movement of the will, divinely made, the human will no longer holds itself purely passively, but being moved, and aided by the Holy Spirit, assents becomes a co-worker with God."

This then is the place at which the Synergism comes into play. The released will made so by grace is a co-worker with God; but the natural will touched by grace works against God. Man may be willing for a beginning which was actually made long ago. Men need not hold back from doing all they can do the salvation of their souls; no, not even if in their short sightedness it looks to them as if they were really beginning the work of their own conversion.

God will take care of that and as their illumination grows they will with increasing clearness that to His Grace they owe great change. He who most earnestly works out his own salvation with fear and trembling will best understand that it is God who worketh in him both to will and to work of his good pleasure.

Chemnitz shows in general the moral nature of this process, following in the statement of Melanchthon. and points out how far we may affirm what see to involve utter helplessness on the part of man. He says "That in the work of conversion man is not as the trunk of a tree, that the carpenter uses an inanimate instrument in one way, but that it is another way in which the Holy Spirit works conversion in the mind, will a heart for He causes it that we wish and are able to understand, to think, to desire and to assent." The instrument of the carpenter has no will, but man bas a will, and by enslaving that will, nor by using its slavery, nor forcing it, but by freeing it, the Holy Spirit produces His saving work. A man with his hands chained cannot co-work with us, nor work in his own unchaining, not at least until the rigidness of his bonds is in part released.

Chemnitz connects with this the stages of conversion in the same way that Augustine had done and Augustinian theology here had been suggested by the experiences of Augustine's own spiritual life.

We have prevenient, preparative, and operative grace. At every step the appropriative power of man is conditioned by the antecedent operation of grace, without which it would not be possible for hi m to appropriate the particular grace successively offered.

These are also the views of the dogmaticians who followed. They bring out very clearly the idea that the acts of the Holy Ghost occurred already in conversion, while the cooperation of the human will first took place after conversion.

This presupposed conversion to be an instantaneous act. Calovius says: "Conversion occurs in a moment in time, *simul ac semel* and as it were in a twinkling of an eye."

Quenstedt indeed traces the steps by which preparation is made for conversion, to wit, by incipient prevenient grace, which removes the natural incapacity of reception; preparatory grace, which controls the resistance of the unregenerate; excitant grace, which uses an external knowledge and a general trust, and finally through the law calls forth the feeling of penitence for past sins- the drawing spoken of in John 6: 44, "No man can come unto me except the Father which has sent me draw him," operative grace, which produces the antecedent of conversion and opens the hearts; perfecting grace, which works and begets 'the acknowledgment of sin and the act of faith.

But with all these distinctions Quenstedt shows that conversion is yet an instantaneous act, so that man's cooperation does not come in until after it, cooperate, he says, "Belongs to the converted man, not to the man who is to be converted." God does not only work so that we can will but he actually do will, as Augustine says.

Quenstedt adds however that: "the first operations of prevenient grace are indeed inevitable but irresistible. We cannot escape them but we can resist them. We cannot avoid having them, in the case supposed, but we can avoid yielding ourselves to them." In these propositions Quenstedt advances beyond Chemnitz. It has been suggested that Quenstedt means to say: "That this grace is of such a character that it is not, in fact resisted, though in its nature it is capable of resistance. The theologians of recent times, especially Julius Mueller, have often maintained that it is impossible to overthrow the doctrine of absolute predestination without attributing to the natural man an independent self-determining relation to divine grace.

To this charge it has been replied by our Lutheran divines (see especially Thomasius), that there is a distinction between our being apprehended by grace and our decision for salvation in the proper sense. The former occurs without the cooperation of man, the second is his self-determining relation which is only rendered possible by the first.

The old dogmatic proposition that "in conversion man is merely passive," must be limited meant to be limited, simply and solely to that point at which the initiation of man's personal salvation is made. We must hold firmly that the work and of our salvation is to be ascribed to God, not to us. "By grace are ye saved, through faith and that not of yourselves, it is the gift of God."

Teaching of Our Dogmaticians.
Definition of Conversion.

Quenstedt: "Conversion is the action of the applying grace of the Holy Spirit, whereby, together with the Father and Son, of absolutely pure grace, founded in the merit of Christ, through the preaching of the Word, He transfers the adult spiritually dead from his state of unbelief to a state of faith, successively as to the preparatory acts, but in an instant as to the ultimate act, by divine supernatural but resistible power, so that, repenting, they obtain by faith the remission of his sins, and partake of eternal salvation."

Usage of Word in a Wide Sense.
Quenstedt: "Conversion is used either in a wide sense as embracing not only transfer from a state of sin to one of faith, but likewise justification and renovation, and the continuation of this new state in its entire extent, Acts 26: 20."
So often in Symbolical Books.

In a Narrow Sense.
Hollaz "Many divines abstain from this extended sense of conversion...but use it in a narrow sense as distinguished from justification and renovation."

Usage in a Special Sense.
Hollaz: "Conversion taken in a special sense is that act of grace by which the Holy Spirit excites the sinner sincere grief for his sins by the word of the Law, and enkindles true faith in Christ by the word of the Gospel that he may obtain remission of sins and eternal salvation."

Here Used in the Most Special Sense.
Hollaz: "Conversion in the most special sense is that act of grace by which the Holy Spirit strains, subdues, and breaks the will and heart of the sinner in the midst of his sins, that he may detest his sins with grief of mind and thus be prepared for receiving faith in Christ." Thus it is the same as intransitive conversion.

Difference Between Transitive and Intransitive Conversion.
Baier: "The word conversion is taken in a double sense in the Scriptures, inasmuch as at one time God is said to convert man, and at another time man id said to convert himself, although as to the thing itself the action is one and the same." The first is called

transitive conversion, because it does not terminate in God who is the agent, but passes from Him to the sinner, and is distinguished as active, so far as it proceeds from God, and as passive, so far as it is received by man. The other is called intransitive conversion.

Definition of Intransitive Conversion.

Hollaz: "Intransitive conversion is the goal and effect of transitive conversion, and is the penitence by which the sinner is said to convert himself by means of the strength imparted by converting grace, and passively received (Acts 3: 19). For which reason the sinner, repenting, converts himself not by his nature, but by imparted powers."

The Starting Point is Sin.

Hollaz: "The starting point is sin, both actual sins...and habitual."

Baier: "That actual sins may be abolished by conversion...they must be recognized by the intellect, not only with a speculative judgment that they are truly sins, but likewise with the practical, that efforts may be made for the abolition of sins;...on the side of the will, efficacious dissatisfaction with sins and a detestation with them united with grief, is required...Conversion tends to abolish habitual sins by the same acts by which it tends to abolish actual sins."

The Grace of God Acts Before Conversion, In it, and After it.

Before conversion the grace of God is called, prevenient, preparative and exciting.

Baier: "By prevenient grace is understood divine inspiration of the first holy thought and godly desire."

In conversion, the grace of God is called operating and perfecting.

Baier: "Operating grace is that which directly follows the commencement of conversion and has reference to its continuance; by which it comes to pass that man's effort, although weak, inclines to Christ, the Mediator and the Promises of gratuitous pardon for Christ's sake, and resists doubts." By perfecting grace the real conversion is accomplished.

After conversion the grace of God is called co-operating, assisting and indwelling grace.

Baier: "Cooperating grace is that operation which aids and strengthens or corroborates the intellect already in some measure assenting to the divine Promises, and the will trusting in Christ, and cooperates with the will, which concurs by the yet weak powers before received."

Quenstedt: "Assisting grace acts exterior to man, and indwelling grace enters the heart of man, changing it spiritually, inhabits it."

The Effect of Grace in Conversion.
Quenstedt: "Grace, effecting and completing conversion by means of the Word, produces

(1) "The knowledge of sin, which is the first stage of conversion;

(2) "Compunction of heart, that there may be testation of sins committed and grief on their account;

(3) "The act of faith itself and confidence in Christ, and the embracing of His merit by true faith; which of faith is immediately followed by a transfer from a state of wrath to one of grace, which is the final act of conversion, and takes place instantaneously, as it cannot be that a man should be in a state of wrath and of grace, under death and in life, at the same time."

Man is Merely Passive in the Beginning of Conversion.
Quenstedt: "In conversion taken in a wide sense, including also the preparatory acts, man is passive in reference to each act or degree; taken in a narrow sense, for transfer from a state of wrath to one of grace, which is instantaneous by means of the gift of saving faith, and in which undoubtedly God alone works, man is also subjected to this divine action as a passive object."

Hutterus: "The conversion of unregenerate believers is one thing, and the conversion of those once regenerated, but now fallen, is another. And there is a great difference between these two kinds of conversion; inasmuch as he who has hitherto been standing in the covenant of divine grace...in some measure is received and possessed the first-fruits of the Holy Spirit and very widely differs from him who for the first time is called and admitted to faith in Christ and the grace in the covenant...Beside these two of conversion, mention is made, in the schools of the divines, of a third kind also, which is called the repentance or conversion of the standing, that is, of those who are regenerate, but who, on account of the adhering iniquities and failings of sin and the flesh, are from time, as it were, revived through repentance...And concerning the two last mentioned kinds, namely, the conversion of the lapsed and of the standing, there is no. controversy or discussion whatever...

"The only question here in dispute is: What can an unbelieving man, hitherto unregenerate, do, by his own strength, in his original conversion?

"To which we reply, that man can do absolutely nothing, not even the very least thing, towards beginning or faith or conversion; and that the beginning, the progress, and in short, the whole development of his conversion is to be ascribed altogether and alone to the operation of the Holy Spirit."

Calovius: "Unregenerate man has, indeed, a passive power, and so a certain aptitude, which should, however, more correctly call a power of resistance, or an obediential power, with respect to his conversion; nevertheless, the Holy Spirit must produce this non-resistance in us, since the nature of man, on count of congenital depraved concupiscence, is in itself hostile to the Holy Spirit, and is not able to refrain from resisting."

The Causes of Our Conversion are Only Two.
Hutterus: "If the question be original conversion, surely neither more nor less conversion can or ought to be assigned than two, those who here add a third, and insist on the will are partakers of the synergistic error...If an unbelieving man who has never been regenerate converted, we assert that only two causes concur, but vastly differing in kind: the one truly efficient, solely and alone the Holy Spirit; the other the instrumental cause, which is the Word of God and heard, as also the right use of the Sacraments.

VI. REPENTANCE.

Conversion begins with the self-judgment of repentance which consists in that change of mind which consummates itself in the knowledge and acknowledgment of sin, in sorrow over sin and in the earnest will purpose to break with sin, in order to live to God.

Scripture Doctrine.
Penitence is the first or negative side, the beginning which lays the foundation for conversion, while faith is the positive side, the final or consummating part of conversion.

Penitence is consequently represented in the Scripture as the internal basis of the new life. Compare the Old Testament the Penitential Psalms, especially Ps. 32 and 51.

The constant demand of the prophets in the Old Testament, is, "Turn ye again now everyone from his evil way," Jer. 25: 5; "Turn unto the Lord," Ps. 22:27. The word "return" is consequently used in general to designate the returning to Jehovah, i.e. conversion. Let it never be forgotten that to convert is simply the Latin for the verb "to turn," and conversion the Latin form of the noun for turning. When Joel says (2: 12) "Turn to me with all your heart" this involves the internal turning away from evil, that is, repentance, Ezek. 3:19, "He turneth not from his wickedness." The verb *nicham* expresses the same great process under the idea of regret or sorrow, Jer. 8; 6, "No man repenteth him of his wickedness." The same idea is presented in a figurative form, Joel 2:13, "And rend your heart, and not your garments, and turn unto Jehovah your God." The outward expression of this internal regret, which must not be confounded with regret itself, is fasting, weeping, mourning, Joel 2:13.

In the New Testament the announcement salvation began with the preaching of repentance (*metanoia*) a noun which the Latin church lathers and) Dogmaticians represented by the Latin words *resipiscentia, mentis emendatio.* This Latin word has the sense of wisdom derived from severe experience, and hence repentance; "Repent ye; for the kingdom of heaven is at hand," Matt. 3:2; "Bring forth therefore fruit worthy of repentance," Matt. 3: 8; "Repent ye; for the kingdom of heaven is at hand," Matt. 4: 17. The burden of John the Baptist's preaching was, "Repent ye"; that is, turn from your false views, turn from your wrong emotions, affections, desires, and acts; bring forth fruits meet for, that is, fitted and appropriate to the great change of mind, heart and purpose, involved in true repentance.

The call to repentance was also part mission of our Lord. The operation which the revelation of salvation was designed to have, was that men should repent in sackcloth and ashes, Matt. 11:21. Over this *metanoia* or repentance, this amendment of head, heart, and life on the part of the sinner, there is joy in heaven among the angels of God, Luke 15: 7, 10.

Repentance is the substance and aim of apostolic preaching; it was the apostolic commission given by our Lord, "That repentance and remission of sins should be preached in His name unto all the nations," Luke 24: 47; and Peter's charge on the day of Pentecost to the inquiring thousands, "Repent ye and be baptized every one you in the name of Jesus Christ unto the remission of sins," Acts 2: 38. In Acts 3: 19 we read, "Repent therefore, and turn again, that your sins may be blotted out."

And Paul in his address at Athens says, "Now God commandeth men that they should all everywhere repent: inasmuch as He has appointed a day, in the which He will judge the world in righteousness by the man whom He hath ordained," Acts 17; 30, 31.

The design of God's goodness is to work repentance, Rom. 2: 4, "not knowing that the goodness of God leads to repentance." God also employs His word of reproof to produce repentance, Rom. 2: 5, "but after thy hardness and impenitent heart treasurest up for thyself wrath the day of wrath and revelation of the righteous judgment of God"; Rom. 3: 3, "For what if some were without faith? Shall their want of faith make of none the faithfulness of God?

God also produces repentance by punishment, which we find a number of illustrations in the book of Revelation, that is, of punishment designed to lead men to repentance, though its aim may be thwarted by their perversity, Rev. 9: 20, 21; Rev. 16: 9, 11.

Repentance is connected with a godly sorrow, and then it is a repentance unto salvation, not to be repented of; that is, the salvation is to be immutable, one in regard to which God changes not, 2 Cor. 7: 10, "For godly sorrow worketh repentance unto salvation, a repentance which bringeth no regret."

Genuine repentance is revealed, first in its internal character. It is a real change of the mind, of the understanding the *nous*, in the mode of thinking, feeling, the affections, the moral inclinations and dispositions. It involves a heart-felt bowing in humility and self-renunciation before God. The publican standing afar off would not lift up so much as his eyes unto heaven smote upon his breast saying, "God be propitiated to me a sinner," Luke 18: 13. The genuineness of it reveals itself in change of life and in the witness of the deed, doing of wrong, the doing of right, as in the case of Zacchaeus, Luke 19: 8, 9.

Church Doctrine.
The Early Church.
Deep and spiritual as are the views of penitence, and perhaps because of their depth and spirituality the Church doctrine upon this very point became, from the time of her decline, exceedingly corrupt. Deadly diseases fixed themselves in vital centers. Penitence was more and more externalized until it went over into the idea of penance, which is a corruption of the word penitence, as the thing called penitence is a corruption of the true thing. It is a corruption leaving its history in a word; and then was made a special sacrament whose object was to supplement baptism, to make propitiation or secure pardon for sins which followed baptism, as baptism wiped out the sins that had preceded it. Prayer, alms, and self-inflicted penalties, were made to contribute to the salvation of the penitent.

Subsequent to the end of the third century there were distinct grades of public repentance or penance for those who on account of grievous sins had been excluded from the Church. These were called grades or stations (*stationes*) of penance.

The first of these was the weeping. The penitent stood at the entrance of the church, imploring with tears, those who entered to give an interest in their prayers to those who were under the excommunication of the church.

The second stage was hearing. At this stage the penitents were allowed, in the company of the unbaptized catechumens, to listen to the exposition of the Scriptures

The third grade or station was the kneeling. They   were allowed to kneel in the nave of the church.

The fourth was the standing up. They were allowed to stand up, during prayer, with the congregation to the end of divine service. The Roman Church has transferred repentance from a relation to God into a relation to the Church.

Teaching of the Roman Catholic Church.

The sacrament of penance consists, according to the Council of Trent of three parts. The first is sorrow, or attrition. By attrition they mean the imperfect the regretting or abhoring of sin because of its eternal penalties; and contrition is the perfect repentance regretting sin because sin is offensive to God, the Romish writers consider attrition sufficient under certain circumstances to secure acceptance with God.

Second is confession before the priest who decides judicially in regard to the sin and the expiation or penance which is to be done for it; and this confession they consider as a necessary act, demanded of God in order to the attainment of sacramental sins.

The third is satisfaction, the *safisfactio operis*, satisfaction of the deed; by which the sinner expiates, atones, offers penance for the temporal punishment of sin, makes restitution, or if he cannot do this to the persons injured, he makes it to the Church, that he may obtain on condition the judicial absolution from everlasting which absolution is given by the priest. The three parts are sometimes stated thus: The contrition of the heart, the confession of the lip, the restitution of the hand.

Luther and the Lutheran Confessions.

It was this externalizing of the profoundest processes of the human heart under the influence of grace which first aroused Luther to set forth in the immortal Ninety-five Theses, over against these corruptions of Rome, true views of penitence. Our Confessions give special prominence to the Scripture doctrine in regard to repentance (A. C. Art. XII; Apol. Chap. V. pp. 178; Chap. VI. pp. 195-213). In presenting the true view of repentance the Apology

(181, 28) says, "We ascribe repentance these two parts, viz. contrition and faith. If anyone desire to add a third, viz. fruits worthy of repentance, i.e. a change of the entire life and character for the better (good works following conversion), we, will not make any opposition." The Variata of the Apology which is often the best of commentaries on the lnvararriata adds, "Neither are we ignorant that with the philologists the word repentance signifies the disapproval of that which we approved before, which suits contrition rather than faith, but for the purpose of teaching, we understand here by repentance the entire conversion in which are the two *termini*, mortification and restoration to life. We call them by the usual names contrition and faith."

The Apology goes on to say: "We say that contrition is the true terror of conscience, which feels that God is angry with sin, and which grieves that it has sinned. And this contrition thus occurs, when sins are censured from the Word of God, because the sum of the teaching of the Gospel is this, to convict of sin, and to offer for Christ's sake the remission of sins and righteousness and the Holy Ghost, and eternal life, and that as regenerate men we should do good works...We therefore, add as the second part of repentance, of faith in Christ, that in these terrors the Gospel concerning Christ ought to be set forth to conscience, in which Gospel the remission of sins is freely promised concerning Christ...This faith cheers, sustains and quickens the contrite according to Rom. 5; 1. This faith obtains the remission of sins. This faith justifies before God, the same passage testifies: 'Being justified by faith'" This last remark was aimed against the Romish doctrine.

It then continues: "And thus filial fear can be clearly defined as such anxiety as has been connected with faith i.e. where faith consoles and sustains the anxious heart. Servile fear is where faith does not sustain the anxious heart."

We see in this extract that our Confession uses repentance in its widest compass, as equivalent to conversion embracing contrition and faith while the word metanoia is used with this same range of meaning in the New Testament, as e. g. Luke 24: 47, "And that repentance and forgiveness of sins should be preached in His name to all the nations"; and Acts 11: 18, "Then to the Gentiles also hath God granted repentance unto life. Yet it is often taken in a narrower sense, and thus taken it is distinguished from faith, thus

Mark 1: 15, "Repent ye, and believe in the Gospel"; Acts 20: 21, "Repentance toward God and faith toward our Lord Jesus Christ

In this narrower sense of the word repentance the Formula of Concord (590, 8) defines it thus, "Repentance means to do nothing else than to truly acknowledge sins, from the heart to regret them, and to abstain therefrom." This definition it gives after speaking of passages in which the Scripture employs it for the whole conversion of man to God. This narrower sense of repentance came to be almost the exclusive one, and repentance came to be distinguished from conversion and from regeneration, while our old dogmaticians almost exclusively employ it in the widest sense as including faith, following in this the usage of the A. C. and Apology.

The A. C. (Art. XII, 3) says: "Repentance consists properly of two parts: One is contrition; that is, terror smiting the conscience through the knowledge of sin; the other is faith, which, born of the Gospel absolution, believes that, for Christ's sake, sins are forgiven, comforts the conscience, and delivers it from terrors."

The Doctrine of Our Dogmaticians.
The doctrine of our dogmaticians is thus stated by Hollaz: "Repentance, as equivalent to intransitive conversion, in which the sinner is said to turn himself, is a movement or emotion of the soul, aroused by the converting and regenerating grace of the Holy Spirit, wherein man, a sinner, being by the law lead to acknowledge his sins, seriously and with grief detest them, and at the same time with true faith lays hold of and applies to himself, the satisfaction and merit of Christ the Mediator, whereby God's pity and promise in the gospel has been attained, so that the free remission of sin being conferred upon him, he is saved forever."

Repentance, taken in its proper separate sense, means contrition a change of mind accompanied with grief; taken in its total sense it means the entire intransitive conversion, i.e. the change of mind which involves both grief and trust.

Repentance may be either that of those who fall, or of those who stand. The repentance of the fallen is either the original conversion of those who have never been Christians, such as is spoken of in 1 Thess. 1:9, "turn to God from idols," or it may be the second repentance of Christians who have fallen, Rev. 2: 5, "Remember therefore from whence thou art fallen, and repent and do the first works." The repentance of those stand is the daily sorrow felt by Christians, over their sins of infirmity.

The two parts of repentance, contrition and faith correspond to the *terminus a quo* of repentance, i.e. sin from which we repent, and the *terminus ad quem*, i.e. the grace of God to which we turn in repentance, from Satan to God. Contrition turns us away from sin, and faith turns us towards the grace of God, and they are spiritual correlatives, one act in two parts or the same act In two aspects, as a physical turning from, must also be a physical turning to. The two parts also correspond a double function of the operative Word of God, as Law and Gospel, contrition being excited by the Law and faith aroused by the Gospel. New obedience is not a part of repentance, but is an effect of it, yet so necessary an effect, that the Apology does not hesitate to allow the close grouping of it with repentance itself. This is opposed to the doctrine of Romanism, Socinianism and Rationalism. Contrition, specially considered, is defined to be a serious and holy grief of heart, in which the sinner lead by the Law to acknowledge his sins abhors and detests them.

The Elements of Contrition.
Gerhard, enlarging upon the particular elements of contrition, makes it embrace six parts: "Contrition embraces
   "1) A true knowledge of sin;
   "2) The sense of the divine anger against sins;
   "3) Anguish and fear of conscience;
   "4) A true humiliation before God;
   "5) Unfeigned confession of sin;
   "6) The serious hatred and detestation of sin."
"Some," he says, "divide contrition according to the faculties of the soul, thus,
   "1) It is in the memory, a recollecting of our sin, a self-reminding;
   "2) It is in the mind, a consideration of our offended God;
   "3) It is in the will, a detestation of acknowledged sins;
   "4) It is in the heart, a fear of judgment to come;
   "5) It is in the conscience, terrified by the thunders of the Law, a feeling of compunction, remorse and grief."
Baier: "The main points in repentance are the acts of the understanding and of the will, the intellectual and the voluntary."

Our old divines, especially over against the Romanists, strongly insist, that the terrors of conscience must form a part of the grief of contrition.

The Objects of Contrition.
The objects of contrition are primarily our actual sins, but in connection with these the innate, or habitual sins also.

The Requisites of True Contrition.
Hollaz: "The requisites of true contrition are antecendently, the knowledge of sin, not only theoretical but likewise practical; formally, an efficacious displeasure or hatred of sin, united with serious grief on account of it.

Contrition is Only a Medium of Salvation.
Over against the Romanists our older divines make these specifications, that "Contrition is neither the meritorious cause of salvation, nor the causal and positive medium of salvation, but is only a medium or means of order, or in the order, that is to say: neither saves us nor is a means of saving us, but as a means it takes its place in order before faith, as a necessary presupposition to faith, just as a consciousness of sickness and a desire to be well is neither the cause of our health nor the means of curing us, but simply, in order comes before the calling of the physician and the use of the remedy. It impels us to seek the cause of healing, and through the appointed means of healing, to be cured."

The Marks of True Contrition.
Hollaz: "These marks are:
"1) Internal
　　"(a) the renunciation of the evil purpose and the omission of the intended sin;
　　"(b) a legal and pedagogic desire for a most approved physician or a most beneficent and powerful deliverer, Acts 2: 37;
"2) External which are discovered;
　　"(a) in the confession of sin, in the mouth of the sinner...before a minister of the Church (Matt: 3: 6), before God (Ps. 51: 3), before a neighbor (James 5: 16);

"(b) in the face and external appearance (tears, sack-cloth, the sprinkling of ashes, smiting of the breast and thigh, rending of garments, lying upon the earth);

"(c) in outward works (fasting and satisfaction, which is rendered to our injured neighbor or to the Church offended by a public scandal)."

Auricular Confession.
Against the doctrine of Auricular confession in its relation to repentance our divines following the A. C. Art. XI, taught that a special enumeration of all and each of our sins with the circumstances, in the presence of the minister of the church is not necessary, "For this," says the Confession, "is impossible, according to Ps. 19: 12, 'Who can discern his errors?'"

Auricular confession is a snare to the conscience, it is the nurse of all abomination, connected as it is in the Church of Rome with the idea of meritoriousness and with repentance itself as an essential of it. It horribly obscures the way to salvation, and while, no doubt, a pure minded and earnest priest might associate with it salutary suggestion, it is in the hands of the great body of the priesthood an instrument of spiritual oppression and of profound demoralization. The Council of Trent requires "secret confession to the priest alone, of all and every mortal sin, of which, upon the most diligent search and examination of our consciences we remember ourselves to be guilty, since our baptism, together with all the circumstances of these sins, which may change the nature of them, because without a perfect knowledge of them the priest cannot form a judgment on the nature and quality of man's sins nor impose fitting penance upon them." Such a confession the Council affirms "to have been instituted by our Lord, and by the law of God to be necessary to salvation and to have been always practiced in the Catholic Church."

In fact the necessity of such a confession to a priest was not established in any institute of our Lord, is not enjoined in His Word, and was contrary to the practice of the ancient Christian Church, and to the earliest practice of the Church of Rome. Confession of sins has indeed always been recognized as a Christian duty. The pastor has always been regarded as under many ordinary circumstances the one to whom a voluntary confession should be made, but such confession as Rome defines and such a necessity as she urges, were utterly unknown in the pure church. There is no proof of the official establishment of auricular confession earlier than the fourth Lateran Council, A. D. 1215. This auricular confession which our Church rejects in Art. XI of the A. C., in the Apol. 176, 63; 177, 64, 65; 197, 13; Smal. Art. 326, 19, is not to be confounded with the private confession, still less with private absolution.

Private Absolution.
In the XI Art. of the A. C. it is said: "Of confession, they teach, that Private Absolution ought to be retained in the church."

It is worthy of remark that in the Article it is not laid down that Private Confession is to be retained, but that Private Absolution is, and the only thing which is made a matter of faith in that Article in regard to Confession is, that in it the enumeration of all our sins is not necessary. This enumeration of sins is necessary to constituting a sort of the very essence of Auricular confession. It is worthy of note furthermore in what sense the word Private is used. The word Private may be used as the opposite of general, and then it has the sense of individual, or it may be used as the opposite of public, or that which takes place in the presence of others. In the first sense we speak of a man's private opinions, private property, private expenses; in the second sense we speak of a private room, private interview, private prayer. Now it is not in the second sense but in the former the word private is used in our confession. Private absolution is that which is given to the individual, and does not necessarily involve privacy in the second sense, that is secret, secreted from the presence of others. Absolution given to an individual, separately from others, is as much private absolution if a thousand people are present, as if there were no one present. Private confession and private absolution are separate things. There is a reason why the Confession among its articles of faith speaks of private absolution and does not mention private confession.

Our church holds that private confession is a merely human ordinance, but it holds that private absolution, i.e. the individual offer to the individual believer, of the divine remission, is a divine ordinance. Private confession may be abandoned at the judgment of the church, but private absolution must in its essence exist while the world stands. Hence in some of our Lutheran churches private confession in its official form is not retained, while private absolution is. That private or individual absolution is actually given in the presence of others, thus in the Lutheran church of Denmark as a preparation for communion there is a general confession in which all the communicants unite in a body; then kneeling around the altar each one receives individually the private or personal absolution, which is connected in the ritual of the church with the laying on of hands.

Private absolution does not in its essence involve a particular form, but whenever a minister of Christ offers to the individual the Gospel promise of pardon to be at once laid bold of by faith, he offers, and where faith receives it, confers absolution by and with the Word, the actual forgiveness of his sins. In the earlier usage of the Church both private absolution and private confession were aided by a form. Confession was regarded as a privilege, as a blessed right on the part of the people. No one was compelled to confess at all; the force brought to bear was purely spiritual. In the Church of Rome, confession at certain times is compulsory, when as a preliminary to communion the members sought the ministry of our Church, it rested entirely with themselves what particular sins they should open to him or whether they should open any. They were encouraged to a free conference with their pastor, to a faithful statement of their spiritual condition, not as a thing necessary to salvation, but as highly salutary. It was made the means of instructing them in sound doctrine, of correcting their mistakes, of preparing them for the Supper of the Lord, of enabling them to realize more perfectly that their sins were forgiven for Jesus' sake, the weak were strengthened, the falsely secure were aroused and those who were burdened in conscience were comforted. It did on system what is done now, if it be done at all, very much at haphazard by pastoral visitation. It is the duty of a Lutheran pastor now as ever, to encourage private confession and private absolution.

Hollaz says: "Private confession, in which are recounted before the minister of the Church sins in general and specifically, the more grievous ones and those which pain the conscience, is rightly retained in the orthodox church, not under the condition of absolute necessity to salvation but on account of its very rich utility."

The Romish Doctrine of Satisfaction.
Finally, over against the Romish doctrine of satisfaction for the temporal punishments which belong to sin, our theologians taught that after sins are forgiven no punishment, properly so called, impends over those who are converted and justified, for punishment is the result of guilt, and consequently when the guilt is taken away the punishment is taken away with it. There remains, however, a fatherly chastening and a curative affliction, Heb. 12: 6; 1 Cor. 11: 32; Rev. 3: 19. It is not the sort of wrath but the keen and necessary instrument of the surgeon which cuts away what is pernicious, which causes the wounds under which God's children may smart.

Repentance Continues Through Life.
Repentance lies in the way of salvation for all men, even to the comparatively few who remain faithful to their baptismal grace. No human being can dispense with it. None but the sinless could cease to need it. In it the personal application of salvation reaches out to its consummation. In this rests the moral character of Christianity. It involves perpetual self-examination, which in the light of God's perfect Jaw involves perpetual self-condemnation.

Repentance is not one short spasm followed by perpetual rest but endures in Christians even unto death, inasmuch as it struggles with sin that remaineth in the flesh throughout our whole life, and this not by our own strength but by the gift of the Holy Spirit, which followeth the remission of sin, and daily prays and casts out the remnants of sin and is ever at work in making man pure, righteous and holy. But the preaching of repentance to those who have been baptized, to whom God already actually stands in a relation of grace, or has stood, must differ from that in which the heathen of heathendom or the heathen of Christendom, are. The mightiest preaching of repentance is that which makes the cross of Christ its center.

VII. FAITH.

The aim of repentance, that to which it tends is that faith which is wrought by the Holy Spirit through the Word of God, which He applies and through which He conveys grace. This faith consummates itself not merely in the intellect or cognitive faculty nor exclusively in the affections, but still more in the will, in the individual and personal appropriation of the salvation wrought out by Christ Jesus and embodied in Him.

Scripture Doctrine.
The Biblical idea of faith is not that of simple assent to propositions, not mere credence, but it means trust and pre-eminently trust which rests upon the God of our salvation.

The Hebrew *aman* properly means to prop up, to sustain, to make firm, as we support with the arm and carry a child. Thus in Num. 11:12 the active participle, means and is translated a nursing-father. The participle corresponds with the Greek *paidagogos* one who carries and cares for a child, Lam. 4: 5. The *Hiphil* has the sense to hold firmly to trust in, to credit, believe in, confide in. It is usually followed by the preposition 6e. The Greek *pisteuein* is equivalent to *pistin echein*, to have faith or trust. The German word is originally *glauben* and has primarily a sense equivalent to *vertreten* in the sense of appearing for, or standing up for, i.e. to confess a conviction and to pledge one's person for it. The English word faith, and parallel words in a number of modern languages, are derived from the Latin fides, which is from *fidere*, to trust. Faith is always an internal thing involving an internal relation.

It is directed to the invisible and supersensuous, and is called in Hebrews 11: 1, *pragmaton elegchos*, translated "the evidence of things." *Elegchos*, however, might be better rendered assured conviction, as *elegcho* from which it is formed is translated by convince. In 1 Cor. 14: 24; Tit. 1: 9; James 2: 9, it is an assurance and confident conviction in regard to the realities which do not pertain to the sphere of sense. It is a conviction, not empirical, depending on our experience as a thing of the sense in the ordinary sphere of knowledge, but is moral, involving an affinity between the subject believing and the object believed. Hence, it is in contrast and in conflict with what seems to be.

It is said of the father of the faithful, that against hope, he believed in hope, Rom. 4: 18. It stands in antithesis to vision, "we walk by faith, not by sight," 2 Cor. 5: 7. Faith in the sphere of religion has to do with God.

In the Old Testament it looked to God through types, prophecies and foreshadowings of Christ. In the New Testament it looks to God through Christ and in Christ as the absolute revelation of God as God, so manifested and revealed that he that has seen Christ has seen the Father, John 14: 9.

The Ground of Faith.

To the questions: "Why are we to have faith?," or "What is the ground of faith?," or "On what authority does our faith rest?" (for faith is always in some sense an acquiescence in authority), the Bible answer is: God, "Wherefore, sirs, be of good cheer: for I believe God, that it shall be even so as it hath been spoken unto me," Acts 27: 25; "Even as Abraham believed God, and it was reckoned unto him for righteousness," Gal. 3: 6.

To believe God is equivalent to believing the word of God, as to believe a man is equivalent to believing what he says. There is no separate affirmation in which the name of Christ is brought in the relation to faith, as the name of God is. But men are represented as believing the word upon the ground that it is Christ's word; John 5: 47, "But if ye believe not his (Moses) writings, how shall ye believe my words?" To this faith our Lord Jesus seeks to draw those who primarily made? His miracles alone the ground of faith, John 2: 23," Many believed on His name, beholding His signs which He did." He makes the appeal, "Except ye see signs and wonders, ye will in no wise believe," John 4: 48, and His aim was to draw them to that sure faith which when asked why it believes, replies, "God has said it."

The Content of Faith.

To the questions, "What does faith?" or "What is the matter or content of our faith?" the answer is, God and Christ are the great matter of our faith. It believes that God is, James 2: 19; that Jesus is the Christ, John 8: 24; John 5: 1, "Whosoever believeth that Jesus is the Christ is begotten of God."

The Aim of Faith.

To the question, "What is the aim and end of faith?" the Scripture answers; that in believing we take to ourselves and give ourselves to God, the God and Savior in Whom we trust, and rest our life forever thereupon.

This aim of faith is involved in the prepositions *eis epi* and *en*. The *eis* marks that our faith is not merely about and toward, but is on, or if the idiom of our language would admit it, into—we believe on Christ, we believe into Christ. The epi has the force of on Christ, and the *en* marks the fixedness of the condition into which we are when we believe into Christ.

The Eleventh Chapter of Hebrews.

This sort of faith, even in the Old Testament, is the fundamental idea of religion. The 11th chapter of Hebrews is the apotheosis of the Old Testament heroes, those of the old dispensation, and they were all heroes of the faith, and the faith of which the Old Testament speaks, and which the 11th of Hebrews illustrates, is not a mere faith in God as almighty, but in Jehovah as the God of salvation. On the ground of His promise, a hope of promise at whose heart lay the hope of the true redemption of Israel, see Luke 2: 38.

The Faith of Abraham.

Such was the faith of Abraham, the type and example of true believers, Gen. 15 and 16. Even in the time of the Law, when the whole fulfillment of the Law was summed up in love, Dent. 6: 5, the basis is faith. "I am the Lord thy God," Ex. 20: 2. The covenant relation is that in which God is the object of that faith which is to produce obedience. So also in the time of the prophets, faith was the presupposition of all salvation. Isa. 7: 9, "If ye will not believe, surely ye shall not be established"; Hab. 2: 4, "Behold, his soul is lifted up, it is not upright in him: but the just shall live by his faith"; 2 Chron. 20: 20, "Believe in the Lord your God, so shall ye be established; believe his prophets, so shall ye prosper."

Faith in the Synoptic Gospels.
From the very outstart faith is presented as the center of conception of the New Testament. The voice that rings out from our Redeemer at the beginning of His mission, His faith preaches and the one demand which involves in its consequences all others, is, "Repent ye, and believe in the Gospel," Mark 1: 15: and the preaching of John the Baptist was but a preparation for Christ's preaching, or rather it was a preaching of faith in anticipation, Mark 1:3, "The voice of one crying in the wilderness, Make ye ready the way of the Lord, Make His path straight."

As the object of this faith Christ designates Himself as the one on whom faith is to bend its gaze and links salvation with it. See Matt. 18: 6, "These little ones which believe on me," Mark 9: 42. The relation of the woman who was a sinner, Luke 7: 37-50; of Zacchaeus, Luke 19: 1-10; of the penitent robber, Luke 23: 40-43, was not other than that of faith in Jesus. This central position and importance is occupied and sustained by faith, in the Gospel of Matthew, just as really as in the Epistles of Paul. The Epistle is but a divine exposition of the Gospel.

Christ's Sermon on the Mount is not meant to put even that exalted fulfillment of the Law which it describes, in the place of faith, but is rather meant to show what sort of fulfillment of the Law a living faith, taught by Christ, yearns so freely to render. The state of heart and mind demanded in the Sermon on the Mount presupposes the personal union with Christ; by faith all in it is expressed (Matt. 5: 11) "for my sake," and this relation to Christ is bound up in the very conception of discipleship toward Him.

After the measure of their faith individuals had part in the salvation of Christ. As they believed so was it done unto them, Matt. 8: 13; 9: 22-29; 15: 28; Mark 5: 34.

Faith in the Usage of St. John.
In the Gospel of John the central signification of faith is unmistakable. It is worthy of note that the noun *pistis* does not occur in the Gospel of John; but the word *pisteuein* occurs more frequently than in all the other three Gospels together. The whole object of the Gospel is summed up in this: "That ye may believe that Jesus is the Christ, the Son of God; and that believing ye may have life in His name," John 20: 31. In every relation of our Lord the Gospel of John depicts that education which He gives to faith,

to a faith which detaches itself from objects of sense and grounds itself upon His Word. They who saw and therefore believed, were reminded of the superior blessedness of those who had not seen and yet had believed, John 20: 29. This faith has Christ Himself in the character of Saviour as the substance to which it clings. In this faith in Jesus Christ, faith in God is consummated. The two are inseparable, "Ye believe in God, believe also in me," John 14: 1.

The elements of faith as depicted in the Gospel of John are the following;

(1) On the side of knowledge it is a beholding, John. 6: 40; 12: 45; a knowing, John 6: 69; 10: 38;

(2) On the side of the will it is a receiving, John 1:12; 3: 11;

(3) With relation to the active powers it is characterized as obedience, hearing the voice, John 10: 16; and its opposite is disobedience non-believing, John 3: 36;

(4) As regards relation, it is spoken of as a personal adhesion, a coming to Christ, a corning to the light. The reproach is: "Ye will not" come to me, that ye may have life," John 5: 40; 6: 35.

The aim of faith in the Gospel of John is represented as internal personal communion, access to the divine through the human, as the eating and drinking of · Christ, John 4: 14; 6: 51; 7: 37. In the 17th chapter the thought is carried out of being in Christ. This communion or oneness with Christ is the fundamental idea of the first epistle of John. Faith in Jesus as the Christ is the true obedience to the will of God, 1 John 3: 23. It is the condition of adoption as children of God, 1 John 5: 1, 2. In short faith is represented as true religion out of which springs true morality, for in this alone is consummated the fellowship with God, 1 John 2: 23. Its opposite is the rejection of God Himself, 1 John 5: 10.

The Teaching of Paul.
Paul emphasizes the moral act of faith as obedience to the faith, Rom. 1: 5. This faith is conditioned by the Word, faith cometh by hearing, Rom. 10: 14-17. It is wrought by God and not by ourselves. It is the gift of God, Eph. 2: 8. It is the result of the operation of God, Col. 2: 12. It is a thing of the heart, the personal center of man, "With the heart man believeth unto righteousness," Rom. 10: 10. Its object is our Lord Jesus Christ. It is on Him, upon Him, and in Him, Acts 20: 21; 1 Tim. 3: 13; or it is called faith of our Lord Jesus Christ,

Rom. 3: 22; Gal. 2: 16, 20. This faith regards the crucified Saviour who has been sent forth as a propitiation through faith in His blood. 1 Cor. 1: 23; 2: 2. Christ who died and is risen again is its object, Rom. 4: 25; 10: 9.

The relation of faith to Christ is expressed grammatically by the use of the dative in one case only, Acts 18: 8, "Believed the Lord," though in 2 Tim. 1: 12 we have the dative of the pronoun. The genitive is more frequently used, Rom. 3: 22; Gal. 2: 16 and in other places. Faith in that which it accepts, is effected by our Lord, so that the faith of Jesus Christ is that of which He is at once the object and the giver. Ordinarily the prepositions are used, sis and epi with the accusative, or pros with the accusative, in the sense of toward. These uses contemplate Christ as the object and aim of faith, and faith as the committing of ourselves to Him. The dative is also employed with *en*, as faith grounds itself upon Christ and rests in Him.

Faith is, consequently, trust, assurance, confidence. We have the full assurance of faith, Rom. 4: 20, 21; 8: 31-39. With this is associated fellowship with Christ. To be in Christ is the fundamental necessity with Paul, in order to be a Christian or, as involving our being in Christ, that Christ be in us, Gal. 2: 20; 3: 26; Eph, 1: 13; 3: 17, "Christ is to dwell in our hearts through faith."

The further development of the doctrine of faith comes in the discussion of the doctrine of justification.

The Church Doctrine.
The Ancient Church.
The history of the doctrine of faith closely coheres with the history of the doctrine of justification, and will be again touched on in that connection. Clemens Romanus still teaches the Pauline doctrine of faith, but, institutes already a parallel between love and faith in his Epistle to the Corinthians (c. 32 and 50).

Ignatius (Eph. 9, 14) says; "The beginning of life is faith, the end is love"; which can be taken in a sense entirely correct.

The power of faith to save is testified to and depicted by Justin Martyr (Dial. c. Trypho, 13, 40, 94, 111, and elsewhere). So also Clemens Alexandrinus, Origen. But there was a tendency more and more to consider faith as a mere intellectual adhesion to Christian truth, and to the doctrine of the Church.

In this same proportion love was exalted. In this manner Augustine conceived of faith as a fundamental act, or basis-laying act of assenting cognition wrought by grace.

The Scholastic Formulation.
On the definition of Augustine rests the Scholastic formulation of stating the doctrine.

Peter Lombard says: "It is one thing to believe in God, another thing to believe God, another thing to believe that there is a God. *Credere Deum* is to believe that there is a God, which the wicked also do. *Credere Deo* is to believe that those things are true which He speaks, which also even the evil do; and we believe a man although we do not believe in the man. *Credere in Deum* is to believe in God; it means in our believing to love Him, in our believing to go to Him, in our believing to cling to Him and to be incorporated with His members."

Corresponding with this was the distinction drawn between *fides informis* and *fides formata*. The *fides informis,* or unformed faith, makes the doctrine of the church merely the object of knowledge and acceptance as true. The *fides formala* is completely formed faith, or shaped by charity or love. Only in the latter sense is faith an act, not merely of knowledge but of will, a virtue and meritorious.

Thomas Aquinas says; "From love which forms faith the soul has it that the will infallibly tends to a good end. And therefore the *fides formata* is a virtue, but the *fides informis* is not a virtue; because although the act of the *fides informis* has the true perfection on the part of the intellect, it has not the due perfection on the part of the will." The act of the will in love was in this way made very prominent. This was united with the cognitive act of assent in order to constitute faith a meritorious virtue. With this view declined the importance which the object of faith has for salvation.

The result was that this object frequently was regarded, not as the distinct fact of redemption as set forth in the New Testament and which is Christ's person and work, but either the invisible world in general or God or the contents of Scripture or the doctrine of the Church.

Aquinas further says: "The object of faith is the primal verity, i.e., divinity." He elsewhere defines the objects as "all things which are contained in Holy Scripture divinely delivered." The considering of the doctrine of the Church, as the object of faith, made necessary to provide for a possible want part of man.

This lead to the distinction between an implicit faith and an explicit faith. "As to the *prima credibilia*,": says Aquinas, "the first things which are to be believed which are articles of faith (such as the Trinity and the incarnation) a man is bound to believe them explicitly, but as regards other truth, he is only bound to believe them implicitly, i.e. his mind is to be prepared to believe anything which Holy Scripture contains." And be adds, "It is manifest that he who adheres to the doctrine of the Church as an infallible rule, assents to all things which the church teaches."

The Protestant Reformation.
Faith is a Personal Relation Towards Salvation in Christ.
The Protestant Reformation came at once in conflict with the scholastic notion of faith. In correspondence with the whole character of the Reformation, faith could no longer be regarded as a mere assent of the truth of the church doctrine or an ignorant presumption of assent to things unknown which might or might not be in the Word of God, but was of necessity apprehended as a personal relation towards the salvation in Christ.

The Apology (p. 91, 48) says; "That faith which justifies, is not merely a knowledge of history, but it assents to the promise of God, in which promise freely, for Christ's sake, the remission of sins and justification are offered. And lest anyone should suppose that it was mere knowledge, we will add further: that it is to wish for and to receive' the offered promise of the remission of sins and of justification."..."But, that faith signifies, not only the knowledge of history, but the faith which assents to the promise, Paul openly testifies, when he says (Rom. 4: 16): 'For this cause it is of faith, that it may be according to grace; to the end that the promise may be sure to all the seed.' For he judges, that the promise cannot be received, unless by faith. Wherefore, he compares them correlatively, and connects promise and faith."

The Formula of Concord likewise says: "Faith is the only instrument by which we can apprehend and receive grace." Faith is consequently not a mere act of knowledge, but one of will. And the Apology adds: "Faith is not only knowledge in the understanding, hut also trust in the will, i.e. a wishing and accepting of that which is offered in the promise."

Faith is an act of the will appropriating salvation wrought by the Spirit and arising from the midst of terror of conscience, and is consequently no idle fancy or pro duct of the mind.

Luther laid great stress upon Christ for us as the great point in faith, the personal communion, the participating with Christ, who is given in faith, he emphasized no less.

The Teaching of Luther.
Luther's view on faith may be thus classified:

Faith is divine.
It is Christian faith when a man believes that he can be justified and saved by no works of his own, and therefore despairs of himself and all his doings, simply hangs on the merits of Christ alone"..."True faith is a certain sure trust of the heart and firm assent, whereby Christ is laid hold on, so that He becomes the object of faith, nay not its object, but as I may" so say, in that faith Christ Himself is present."..."Faith lays hold of Christ and has Him present and grasps Him to itself as the bridal ring grasps the jewel."

Relation of Faith to Repentance.
The first part of repentance is to fear God, etc. The second is faith. In substance this view is identical with the Augsburg Confession.

Distinction in Faith.
Luther distinguishes justifying faith from historical faith. And he distinguishes between abstract faith and incarnate faith.

Faith is sometimes taken apart from works, sometimes with works. For an artificer speaks in various ways of his workmanship, and as gardener talks about his trees; either simply as a tree or a bearing fruit; so also the Holy Spirit in Scripture speaks in various ways about faith.

Sometimes it speaks of what I shall call abstract or absolute faith; sometimes about concrete, composite or incarnate faith. It is absolute or abstract faith when the Scripture is speaking absolutely concerning justification or justified persons, as in the Epistle to the Romans and Galatians. But when the Scripture is speaking of rewards and punishment of works, then it speaks of faith composite, concrete, or incarnate. Such sentences are these: "This do and thou shalt live"; "If thou wouldst enter into life, keep the commandments"; "Depart from evil and do good."

Luther distinguishes also between true and false faith. "We distinguish between true faith and feigned faith. Feigned faith is that which hears about God, Christ and all the mysteries of the incarnation and redemption and apprehends those things that are heard and knows how to talk about them very beautifully, and yet remains mere opinion and empty hearing, In very deed, however, this is not faith, for it does not renew nor change the heart, does not generate the new man, but leaves man in his old way of thinking and course of life.

... And this faith is exceedingly pernicious. It would be better not to have it at all. A philosopher of moral life is better than a hypocrite who has this faith."

Luther sums up in these words; "It was done for thy sake and for thy good. He is our Saviour and died and rose for us...Historical faith does not rest upon, nor trust in the Word, but says—'I hear that Christ suffered and died'—but true faith thus thinks—'I believe that Christ suffered and died for me.' Concerning it I doubt not, and I rest in that faith, and I trust in that Word against death and sin."

Relation to Regeneration and Sanctification.
"Through faith we are regenerated, not alone to hope of eternal life, but to righteousness and a new life. In this new life, being instructed by the Word we are diligent by the help of the Holy Ghost in being obedient to God...Through the faith of Christ we are not free from works, but from opinions of works, i.e. from foolish presumption of justification to be sought through works. For faith redeems our consciences, makes them right and preserves them. Know that righteousness is not in works, though neither can be, nor ought to be absent."

Faith is not a Work, but the Witness and Life of works.
"The sophists when they hear us teach concerning faith think that a trifling matter is involved, for they know not that faith is a change and renewal of the whole nature, so that the ears, the eyes, the heart, hear, see, and perceive wholly diversely from those of all other men; for faith is a living and mighty thing. It is not empty

thinking, nor does it float upon the heart as a fowl upon the water, but is as water heated, which indeed remains water, yet is cold no longer."

The Power of Faith is Derived from Christ on Whom It Lays Hold.
"It is not the christian who speaks, who works, who suffers, but Christ in him. All his works are works of Christ, so priceless is the grace of faith...faith is to be purely taught, because through it thou art so found together with Christ, that of thee and Christ there becomes, as it were, one person who is inseparable, so that with confidence thou canst say. 'I am Christ', i.e. Christ's righteousness and victory and life is mine', and again Christ saith, 'I am that sinner i.e. his sins and death are mine, for be clingeth to me and I to him, for we are conjoined through faith into one flesh and bone.'" A volume of rich matter might be made from Luther's utterance in regard to faith. He constantly dwells upon the thought that faith is not a dead affection or quality, but a great work and movement of the Holy Ghost.

"Faith" says Luther, "i.e. the science and wisdom of the things of darkness and the things of naught, i.e. it has to do with things which do not appear and are almost impossible."

He quotes the powerful expression of Bernard in regard to the Virgin Mary, who says, "the faith of Mary that she was to be the mother of Christ was no less a miracle than the Incarnation itself."

One of the most necessary and glorious parts of the work of the Reformation was to restore the true idea of faith as involving a personal relation toward the salvation in Christ. It must be no bare historical notion, but an assenting to the promise of God, in which freely, for Christ's sake, remission of sins and justification are offered.

The Nature and Quality of Faith.
Faith is a willing and an accepting; it is special or specific; every man must have it for himself believing that his sins are forgiven, for Christ's sake. Faith is the sole instrument by which we can lay hold of grace. It is a work of the Holy Spirit; it frees from death; it brings forth new life; it cannot exist with willful sin; it brings forth good fruit by the law of its being. It cannot be given to those who never felt the true contrition, or to those who have the purpose of

persevering in sin. Penitence precedes it; holiness follows it; it has its power not as a merit, but, as a means of grasping all merit, in grasping Christ. It is in the understanding, with respect of the knowledge of God, and in its trusting assent to God in that knowledge. It is in the will with respect to trust. It goes forth to God; and rests on Him. The general object of faith is the whole revealed word of God; but the object of specific or saving faith is Christ, the Mediator.

The Parts of Faith.
The parts of justifying faith are three: (1) knowledge, (2) assent, (3) trust. Rather is it trust however, which presupposes knowledge and assent.

Trust is an act of the will wherein the converted and regenerate sinner earnestly seeks the mercy of God obtained by the merit of Christ, and embraces this as the cause of the remission. of sins and eternal salvation and joyously and securely rests in it. This trust is the acceptance, the apprehension or laying hold or appropriating the merit of the Godman, each individual bringing it to himself. It involves a resting of the whole heart and will in the merit of Christ.

This trust is the grand element in the essential nature of faith. Justifying faith is the receptive organ, it is the hand of the soul, the hand moved by divinely given power by which it receives and applies grace to itself. Grace is the hand of God which holds forth the treasure of righteousness and salvation in Christ. Faith is the band of the soul which grasps and receives the offered treasure. The instrumental cause of faith is the word and sacraments. Faith in the baptized infants is a divinely wrought condition, it is the State which underlies the act, and as a child is by nature a sinner before it can commit conscious acts of sin; so is it by grace rendered a believer before it can put forth conscious acts of faith.

The Operation of Faith is Twofold.
It is receptive; or it is active and working. Justifying faith is simply receptive. It is not the good work of a good worker, but the receptive band of a helpless beggar. Active or operating faith is the faith of a justified man, the beginning of a new life. To justifying faith belongs normally assurance. He, in whom faith trusts, should

be fully trusted, and he who trusts should fully trust; and when these elements conspire there is the lull assurance of faith.

Full Assurance of God' s Mercy.
It is possible to know that we are converted and renewed, and have the forgiveness of sins, and the chief evidence of this to ourselves is the work of the indwelling Spirit of God. In the Church of Rome it is denied that man can have the full assurance of divine mercy except by a special revelation of God. The distinction between the Romish and the Evangelical view in regard to faith has been clearly stated by Bellarmine.

Romanism and Lutheranism differ in three points in regard to the notion of faith. (1.) In regard to its object, we hold it to refer to the promise of God's special mercy; the Romanists make it to cover the whole Word of God. (2.) We collocate it in the will, the Romanists locate it in the understanding (3.) We define it as trust; the Romanists as assent.

The Teaching of our Dogmaticians.
Individual Elements of Faith.
Faith, with reference to its individual elements, consists in knowledge, assent, and confidence.

Baier: "Knowledge is commonly regarded as the first step of faith, or the first part or the beginning of faith. There must be explicit knowledge of things to be believed, especially concerning Christ and His merit, concerning the grace of God, or the salvation to be obtained thereby from God. That knowledge is necessary to faith in Christ, is proved by John 6: 69; 17: 3; 1: 77; Acts 17: 23, 30; Eph. 4: 18; Gal. 4: 9."

Quenstedt: "The second act of faith is assent which is more distinctive than knowledge, for even heretics may have knowledge and yet not yield assent to the, "Word known. But this assent is not superficial, doubting, vacillating, but should be decided and strong on which account it is called the evidence of things not seen, Heb. 11: 1. This act of faith does not depend upon the evidence of things, or upon a knowledge of causes and properties, but upon the infallible authority of God's Word."

Hollaz: "Confidence is an act of the will, by which the sinner, converted and regenerate, earnestly desires and seeks the mercy of God, secured by Christ's merit, and embraces Him both as his own present good, and as the cause of the forgiveness of sins and of eternal salvation, relies upon Him against all terrors, and securely reclines and rests upon Him."

Quenstedt: "Thus confidence is nothing else than the apprehension of the merit of the Godman, appropriating it to ourselves individually. (The following passages indicate the apprehension, John 1: 5, 12; 17: 8; Rom 5:17; Gal. 3: 14; Luke 8: 13; Acts 8: 14; James 1: 21; Acts 10; 43; 1 Tim. 1: 15. Appropriation is indicated by the applicative and possessive pronouns my, me, mine, as is evident from Job. 19: 25; Is, 45: 24; John 20: 28; Gal. 2: 20, 21)...It belongs, therefore, to confidence to apprehend Christ with His righteousness, Rom. 9: 30; to embrace Him with all acceptation, 1 Tim. 1: 15; to appropriate His merit to oneself, Gal. 3: 26; Phil. 1: 21; and sweetly to rest in Him, Rom. 4: 21; Heb. 10: 22. This apprehension belongs to the will and is practical; it involves the reclining of the whole heart and will upon the merit of Christ; it denotes desire for and access to Christ, and the application and confident appropriation of His merit. And this is truly confidence."

Difference between Implicit and Explicit Faith.
A mere implicit faith, such as says that it believes what the church believes, although he has no knowledge whatever as to what these things are which the church believes, is not sufficient, but there must be an explicit faith.

Baier: "Explicit faith is that by which the thing to be believed, although it be not clearly known, or although all the things in it that are cognizable be not intelligently apprehended, yet is in itself known distinctly, or in such a manner, that it can be distinguished from other objects."

Distinction Between General Assent and Special Assent.
Hollaz: "By general assent, the universal promises of the grace of God and the merit of Christ are regarded as true. By special assent, the converted, regenerate sinner regards these general promises as pertaining to him individually. In 1 Tim. 1: 15, the general and special assent of faith are united...that they may become actually profitable to one or another individual, it is necessary that the universal merit of Christ, and the indeterminate promises, should

be applied and determined by special assent to this or that penitent sinner."

Definition of Faith.
Hollaz: "Faith in Christ is the gift of the Holy Spirit, by which the converted and regenerated sinner savingly recognizes, with firm assent approves, with unwavering confidence applies to himself, the gospel promise of the grace of God and of the forgiveness of sin and eternal salvation, to be obtained through the atonement and merit of Christ, so that he may be justified and eternally saved."

Distinction Between General and Special Faith.
Hollaz: "General faith is that by which man, who needs salvation, believes all things to be true which are revealed in the word of God. Of this species of faith we are not now speaking, but we wish to speak of special faith. This is that kind of faith by which the sinner is converted and regenerated, applies to himself individually the universal promise in reference to Christ, the Mediator, and the grace of God accessible through Him, and believes that God desires to be propitious to him and to pardon his sins, on account of the satisfaction of Christ, made for his and all men's sins...Justifying or special faith presupposes and includes general faith...Justifying or special is the receptive organ and, as it were, the hand of the poor sinner, by which he applies and takes to himself, lays hold of, and possesses those things which are proffered in free promise of the gospel...the sinner, in the abyss of misery, receives, as a beggar, in his hand of faith, what is thus offered to him. The offer and the reception are correlatives. Therefore, the hand of faith, which seizes and appropriates the offered treasure, corresponds to the hand of grace which offers the treasure of righteousness and salvation."

God is the Principal Efficient Cause of Saving Faith.
Quenstedt: "This is evident from John 6: 29; Phil. 1: 29. Hence faith is called the gift of God, Eph. 2: 8, and it is said to be of the working of God, Col. 2:12. This shows that faith proceeds from God, who regenerates, and is not the product of our own will; it is not meritorious. It has its origin in grace, not, in nature; it is supernatural, not natural. Faith is of God in its beginning, Phil. 1:

6; 2: 13, in its increase, Mark. 9: 24; Luke 17: 5; and in its completion, Phil. 1: 6; 2 Thess. 1: 11."

The Instrumental Cause of Faith.
Gerhard: "God does not wish to produce faith in the hearts of men immediately, or by enthusiastic raptures of the Holy Spirit, but mediately by the preaching, hearing, and reading of the Word, and meditation upon it. Therefore the instrumental cause of faith is the preaching of the Word. The Holy Spirit not only offers in the Gospel the vast benefits procured by the passion and death of Christ; but operates also through the Word upon the hearts of men, and kindles in them faith by which they embrace and apply to themselves the proffered mercies."

Quenstedt: "The conferring means in adults are, first, the Word preached, heard, and devoutly considered, John 17: 20; Rom. 10: 17; 1 Cor. 1:21; 2 Cor. 4: 6; and afterwards the Sacraments. In infants, however, Baptism is first as a source generating faith."

Distinction between Direct and Discursive Faith.
Hollaz: "We distinguish faith in relation to the mode of knowledge, as direct, which directly leads to Christ and the grace of God afforded in Him, e. g. infants believe, and have direct faith, but they cannot prove their faith, for want of ripened judgment, and reflex and discursive faith, by which a man regenerated believes and perceives that he believes, so that he can say with Paul, 2 Tim. 1: 12: 'I know whom I have believed.'"

Distinction Between Dead and Living Faith.
Hollaz: "A dead faith is only an empty persuasion and boasting of faith, or a bold presumption upon the mercy and grace of God on account of the merit of 'Christ, in an impenitent man, indulging himself in sin.

Concerning this, see James 2: 20. We speak of true and living faith, which receives its vitality from Christ and when it justifies the converted sinner and exerts and displays its vital energy in love and good works."

The Apology says: "Faith is dead which does not produce good works: living, that which does produce them."

Distinction Between Receptive and Operative Faith.

The distinction of Hollaz is very striking: "The power and energy of faith are twofold, receptive, or apprehensive, and operative. The former is that by which faith passively receives Christ and everything obtained by His merit, John 1: 12; 17: 8; Col. 2: 6; 1 Tim. 1: 15; Rom. 5: 17; Acts 10: 43; James 1: 12; Gal. 3: 14. The latter or operative is that by which faith manifests itself actively by works of love and the practice of other virtues, Gal. 5: 6...The epithet, working through love, Gal. 5: 6, is an attribute of faith which has justified, not of one which will in the future justify, much less the form or essence of justifying faith as far as it justifies."

Brenz: "Faith, so to speak has two hands. One, which it extends upwards to embrace Christ with all His benefits, and by this we are justified; the other, which it reaches downwards to perform the works of love and of the other virtues, and by this we prove the reality of faith, but are not thereby justified."

Distinction Between Weak and Strong Faith.
Hollaz: "Faith is weak or infirm, when either a feeble light of the knowledge of Christ glimmers in the intellect, or the promise of grace is received with a languid and weak assent, or confidence struggles with an alarmed conscience. So Mark 9: 24. But yet a weak faith may be true; as a spark concealed under the ashes is true fire, and a tender infant is a true human being. A strong and firm faith is a clear knowledge of the divine mercy, offered in Christ, a solid assent, and intrepid confidence overcoming all terrors. See Rom. 4: 18."

Chemnitz: "The essential should be marked, for we are justified by faith not because it is a virtue so firm, robust, and perfect; but on account of the object, because faith apprehends Christ. When then faith does not err in its object, but apprehends that true object, although with languid faith, or at least endeavors and desires to apprehend it, it is genuine and justifies."

Certainty belongs to Faith in Christ.
Hollaz: "1) On the part of the object believed, in which there can be no falsehood. For the Word of God, which is received by the assent of faith, is most true, on account of the authority of God who reveals it.

"2) On the part of the subject, or of him who believe and who most firmly adheres to and depends upon the divine promises.

For faith is the evidence of things and seen, Heb. 11: 1; a firm assent and a full confidence Rom. 4: 21; Col. 2: 2: Heb. 6: 11; a firm persuasion Eph. 3: 12; 1 Cor. 6: 17."..."Converted and regenerated men can and do know with an infallible certainty, that they truly believe, both from the concurring testimony of the Holy Ghost with the testimony of their own spirit, or of their soul enlightened and renewed (Rom. 8: 16; 1 John 5: 9), and likewise from the examination and proof of faith (2 Cor. 13: 5)."

Various Statements in Regard to Faith.
Quenstedt: "If you inquire after the origin of justifying faith, it is heaven-derived; if in regard to the means by which it is proffered, it is begotten by the Word of God and the Sacraments;

"If in regard to the effect, it attains the pardon of sins;

"If in regard to the consequence, they are shown through the holy works of love;

"If in regard to the reward, it is recompensed in eternal salvation;

"If in regard to the relation to virtues, it is the root and foundation of the rest."

JUSTIFICATION.

The consequence of faith, in the grace of God in Christ is justification. Justification is an act of the divine mind; it is a judgment or decision of God, in conformity with which God especially and individually, imputes and applies to the sinner the propitiation which Christ has wrought, and in consequence of this, for Christ's sake, absolves him from all the guilt and penalty of sin, and receives him into His favor. Of this new relation in which God has placed the sinner to Himself, He testifies inwardly by the spirit of adoption and fits him by that spirit for the new position of childlike devotion.

Scripture Doctrine.
The Old Testament presents in its facts the New Testament's doctrine of justification. From the beginning of the history of man, in God's promise, was the condition of acceptance with God and the bond of man's entire fellowship with God, (Abel, Enoch and Abraham, Heb. 11). In the time of the Law, though outward obedience was strictly enjoined, two ideas, were never last sight of, 1) that the state of a believing heart is essential to any real fulfilling of the law; 2) that the law never was so fulfilled as to enable a man to put his trust in anything but the forgiving mercy of God.

Dikaios, what is right, conformed to right, just, is synonymous with *agathos*, good, only that *dikaios* is a conception of a relation, and presupposes a norm, whereas the subject of *agathos*, is his own norm, so that *agathos* includes the predicate *dikaios*.

As to the import of the conception in a mar sense, there is a decisive difference, not to be mistaken between the Greek usage and the Biblical, and this difference arises from the opposite standards by which it is estimated in the two spheres. Righteousness in the Biblical sense is a condition of rightness, the standard of which is God, which shows itself in behavior conformable to God, and has to do above all things with its relation to God, and with a walk before Him. Righteousness in the Scripture is thus a thoroughly religious conception, designating the normal relation of men and their acts, to God. Righteousness in the profane mind is and remains a social virtue, only with a certain religious background;

In the New Testament, faith is constantly presented as the condition of salvation in Christ. The repentance for the remission of sins is one whose vital part is faith. The new righteousness which the Gospel proclaims is a gift of God, who justifies man through grace, by not imputing to him his sins, on the ground of the suffering and death of Christ, and by imputing to him the righteousness which was obtained for the believer by the complete fulfillment of the Law by Christ. The fundamental doctrine of justification by faith is most fully discussed in the Epistles to the Galatians and to the Romans.

In the last Epistle it is the leading theme (Rom. 1: 16, 17). After the apostle bas shown that it is impossible of oneself, by means of the works of the Law, to attain to righteousness that avails before God, he continues in 3: 21, 22, thus: "But now apart from the law a righteousness of God hath been manifested—even the righteousness of God through faith in Jesus Christ unto all them that believe."

This is not a righteousness of our own, which we have earned ourselves, but a righteousness which is of God, because He alone bestows it (Rom. 10: 3), and He alone procures it for us (1 Cor. 1: 30). It is a gif t, a free bestowment of God's grace (Rom. 3: 24; 6: 23). It is this righteousness which is now proclaimed in the Gospel (Rom. 1: 16, 17), as being brought about by means of the death of Christ (2 Cor. 5: 21). It is guaranteed through Christ as the Mediator, His death and resurrection forming the condition (Rom. 4: 24, 25; 5: 9).

But four questions here come under consideration: 1) What is the meaning of the expression to justify? 2) In what does justification itself consist? 3) What is the condition of justification? 4) What is the nature of true faith that justifies?

1) It is evident that Paul always uses the word *dikaioun*, "to justify," in the sense of esteeming, pronouncing, accounting, treating as righteous, both according to the measure of the law (Rom. 2: 13; 3: 20), and also according to grace. And in the whole

discussion of the Epistle to the Romans and Galatians the justification of the sinner before God is the theme-that man, although not justified by the law, is esteemed and treated as righteous by God. In all these passages, the fundamental meaning of to justify is the forensic and juridical signification, to account as righteous. The contrast of "to justify" is "to accuse" (Rom. 8: 33). The antithesis of justification is condemnation (Rom. 5: 18). Whosoever is not justified is liable to punishment and under the curse (Gal. 3: 10, 11; Rom. 10: 13). From all this there can be no doubt as to the forensic character of the justify" as used by Paul.

The opposite interpretation, which understands "to justify" as making righteous, has been brought forward by the Rationalists, by the Roman Catholic Church, and by such Protestants as blend justification with sanctification, and connect the former not with faith, where it rightly belongs, but with love and good works.

2) If we examine more closely the divine act of justification we find it involves two things:

a) Sin is not imputed to the sinner as guilt or in other words he receives forgiveness of sins (Rom. 4: 5-8; Gal. 3: 11, 13; see also Acts 13: 38, 39). We may call this the negative side of justification.

b) The second part in justification consists in the imputation to the believer of the righteousness obtained by Christ through His fulfilling the law. This reckoning of righteousness unto the believer is the positive side of justification (Gal. 2: 21; 3: 21, 27; Rom. 4: 11).

Our peace (Rom. 5: 1) is conditioned on these two points. We are thus reconciled to God (Rom. 5: 10, 11; 2 Cor. 5: 20), and have the assurance of the divine love to us (Rom. 5: 5). We know ourselves to be sons of God (Rom. 8: 14-17; Gal. 4: 6, 7). Justification is therefore both an act of God, and the atonement of Christ rendered subjective and brought to consciousness.

3) God has appointed the condition under which He justifies the sinner. This condition is faith, (Rom. 3: 22; 10: 4; Acts 13: 39). The righteousness of God is attained and appropriated by faith (Rom. 1: 17; 5: 1), even through faith (Rom. 3: 22, 25, 30). Or to speak more accurately, faith is the condition of justification or righteousness (Rom. 9: 30; 10: 6); or, to express it in another way, justification is attained upon the occasion of faith; for the new righteousness is a righteousness which is of faith (Rom. 4: 11, 13; 10: 10).

This act of God in the matter of justification is by no means an absolutely new one. It is not only borne witness to prophetically in the Old Testament, hut it has already found its typical precedent in the history of Abraham. According to Gen. 15: 6, Abraham believed, and his faith was reckoned unto him for righteousness (Gal. 3; 6; Rom. 4: 3).

4) Equally clear is the statement what Paul regards as the nature of true faith. In Paul's view faith is the confident grasping and holding fast of Jesus Christ, which presupposes a renunciation of one's own sufficiency, and is an entry into the fellowship with Christ. The Pauline faith is not a mere honesty of conviction. It is not a mere theoretical, or an historical knowledge of Christ, and a sure belief in the Gospel, but a lively inward apprehension of Christ and His Gospel. Now, since justification is brought about by means of the atoning death of Christ, faith may be described in various ways, as a faith which is grounded upon Christ (Rom. 10: 14; Col. 2: 5; Phil. 1: 29), or, as a faith which rests in Christ (Gal. 3: 26; Col. 1: 4; Eph. 1: 15), or, as a trust in Christ (Rom. 3: 22, 26; Gal. 2: 16; 3: 22). Faith is, therefore, the humble acceptance of the gift of Grace offered by God.

Where there is true faith, all three elements of faith (knowledge, Gal. 4: 9; 3: 23; 2: 2; assent, Gal. 1: 6, 8, 11, 12; 2: 14; and trust, Gal. 2: 16; 3: 26) must be present; but confidence or trust in Christ is the principal part of faith.

We must repeat here that the power and energy of true faith are twofold, receptive and operative. Faith, so to speak, has two hands. One, which extends upwards passively to receive Christ and everything obtained by His merit (Gal. 3: 14, 22; 2; 16), and by this we are justified; not, however, as the ground of our justification, for this is the atoning death of Christ; nor as the cause; of our justification, for this is the abounding mercy of God; nor as the means by which grace is conferred upon us, for this is done by means of the Word and Sacraments, but simply as the means whereby forgiveness of sins is accepted.

The other hand, which reaches down ward to perform works of love, is known as operative faith and it manifests itself by works of love (Gal. 5: 6, 14, 22: 6: 10), and by this we prove the reality of faith, but are not thereby justified.

The Pauline doctrine of justification as developed in the Epistles to the Galatians and the Romans is also expressed very precisely in the Epistles of the First Captivity (Colossians, Ephesians, Philippians). So Eph. 2: 8, 9, we find the true Pauline antithesis, "For by grace have ye been saved through faith; and that not yourselves: it is the gif t of God: not of works, that no man should glory." So likewise Phil. 3: 8, 9, "I count all things to be lost for the excellency of the knowledge of Christ Jesus my Lord, that I may gain Christ, and be found in Him, not having a righteousness of mine own, even that which is of the law, but that which is through faith in Christ, the righteousness which is of God by faith."

Some suppose that there is a real contradiction between the doctrinal systems of James and Paul, and that James wrote for the express purpose of correcting the Pauline doctrine. The true solution lies in considering the following points:

1) We have most convincing internal evidence that the Epistle was written by James before 50 A. D., at least prior to any book of the New Testament, and prior to the writings of Paul. The early date of the Epistle is implied by the indirect notices of church organization and church discipline. No mention is made of bishops, but only of teachers and elders (3:1; 5:14), which were also recognized in the synagogue. The church (5:14) probably still worshipped in the synagogue (2: 2). There is no allusion whatever to the great controversy concerning circumcision and the observance of the Mosaic law. This question had not as yet arisen.

2) There is therefore no reference whatever, either directly or indirectly, in the argument of James, to the Pauline argument. The two lines of argument as presented by the two writers, being aimed at totally different errors, neither cross nor touch each other.

3) In James 2: 14-26 the Apostle warns those who, having been regenerated and justified (1:18, 21, 25; 2:1), are now leading a lifeless profession of orthodoxy, irrespective of moral conduct, without compassionate love (2:8, 9, 16), that such an idle, barren faith (2:20) is dead (2:26), yes, dead in itself (2:17), utterly without avail in the sight of God, at the time that men shall be judged by the Gospel, the law of liberty (2:12)— in fact, such a faith professed by them is not that faith which triumphs and saves in the day of judgment (2:13). James is but enforcing the same truths taught so forcibly by Christ Himself, "By their fruits ye shall know them. Not everyone that saith unto me, Lord, Lord, shall enter into the kingdom of heaven; but he that doeth the will of my Father which is in heaven" (Matt. 7: 20, 21); "I say unto you, that every idle word

that men shall speak, thee shall give account thereof in the day of judgment. For by thy words thou shalt be justified and by thy words thou shalt be condemned" (Matt. 12: 36, 37); "The word that I spake the same shall judge them in the last day" (John 12: 48).

4) James therefore does not deny the glorious Pauline doctrine of justification by faith nor has he denied in 2: 14; he in fact explicitly grants that righteousness reckoned through faith in the strict Pauline sense, "For Abraham believed God, and it was reckoned unto him righteousness; and he was called the friend of God" (2: 23); but what James wishes to make clear is, that at the time of judgment, in the day when final salvation will be awarded (2: 12, 13), whether at the particular judgment which overtakes every individual at death, or at the final judgment at the last day, which is but the final completion of a process definitely determined at the moment of death, then such professed faith in which these Pharisaic Jewish Christians pride themselves will not avail before God, "For at the righteous judgment of God, He will render to every man according to his works" (Rom. 2:6).

St. Paul in Romans discusses the question, how shall a sinner be justified, and his answer is by faith alone, by faith apart from works of the law (Rom. 3; 28). In the Epistle of St. James the question is not how is a man justified, but how does that faith which justifies man prove itself not to be a hollow pretense, but a real divine power. How shall a man claiming to be a saint be justified in that claim before the world and at the judgment day, at death? The answer is in general, it justifies itself and proves that a man bas faith by the good works it brings forth and his answer is the true one. A man is not cured by the marks of health—the cure must precede these-and these if there were no cure would be illusive. But when we ask how does the reality of the cure prove itself? we answer by the marks of health. Faith heals the soul; and works of a new obedience testify to the healing; so we may say that though the marks of health do not produce health, yet where there are no marks of health, there is no health.

The Church Doctrine.
The Early Church.
In a clear doctrinal apprehension, the Pauline doctrine was soon lost; but as involved in the real spiritual life, it abode in the Church always, even when the formulation of the doctrine seemed most

adverse to it. With the confusion which grew up in regard to the true idea, there grew up of necessity, a false idea of the nature of justification.

The Middle Ages.
In the middle ages there was a constant growth of a Pelagianizing view of the merit of human nature, yet even then were many touching proofs that the Holy Spirit could reach the hearts of men with the power of that very truth, which seemed everywhere ignored and rejected.

The Reformation.
The Reformation, in the restoration of faith to its true place, lifted the Church to a profounder and intenser consciousness of the nature of justification, than it ever had possessed. It was on justification that the battle against Rome was fought.

Teaching of the Lutheran Confessions.
The Augsburg Confession (Art. IV) says, "Our churches teach, that men cannot be justified before Go by their own strength, merits or works, but are freely justified for Christ's sake through faith, when they belief that they are received into favor and that their sins are forgiven for Christ's sake, who, by His death, has made satisfaction for our sins. This faith God imputes for righteousness in His sight. Rom. 3 and 4."

This doctrine of justification was the chief topic, upon which our Confessions laid stress. It is the central article, primary and principal. It can neither be yielded, nor softened; losing it all is lost.

Osiander (d. 1554) identified justification with the internal fellowship of life with Christ, and transmuted Christ for us, into Christ in us.

Stanoarus (d. 1574) taught that our justification is based solely upon the obedience of Christ according to His human nature.

Against both these errorists the Formula of Concord (p. 501) teaches that "the entire Christ according to both natures, alone by His obedience, which as God and. man He rendered the Father even to death, merited for us the forgiveness of sins and eternal life, as it is written in Rom. 5: 19." It further teaches that our salvation is based upon the imputation of Christ's righteousness; faith alone is the instrument by which we lay hold of Christ; that this faith is not an intellectual act, but assent and trust; that justification is not a making righteous but a declaring of the forgiveness of our sins, and a treating us as if we were righteous; that we are firmly to rest in our undoubting assurance of our salvation.

That the exclusive particles be retained with a special care, as when the holy apostle Paul writes, "of grace," "without merit," "without works," "not of works"—that all these words, taken together, mean that "we are justified and saved alone by faith in Christ" (Eph. 2: 8; Rom. 1: 17; 3: 24; Gal. 3: 11); that though the contrition that precedes, and the good works that follow do not belong to the article of justification, yet that no justifying faith can be imagined as co-existing with a wicked intention to sin and to act against conscience, but that after man is justified by faith, then a true genuine faith worketh by love (Gal. 5: 6); that thus good works always follow justifying faith, and are surely found with it, if it be true and living; for it never is alone, but always has with it love and hope.

General Statement of the Teaching of the Dogmaticians.
The dogmaticians developed this doctrine with peculiar power. They show that justification is an act of grace, of pure pity, made possible in its exercise by the satisfaction and merit of Christ. It is laid hold of by the true faith. It involves forgiveness of sins and imputation of Christ's righteousness, the adoption as God's children and the inheriting of eternal life. To justify is not a physical term; it involves not in itself a change of nature; but it is a forensic term, drawn from legal usage, meaning to absolve, to pronounce free from condemnation and penalty, to acquit. Justification is an act in the view and judgment of God. In itself it is entirely in God. It does not take place in man and hence in itself can involve no intrinsic change in man. The father's pardon of a guilty son takes place in the father's heart and in itself implies no change in the son.

The *efficient cause* is grace, pity, the free favor of God. The *meritorious cause* is the satisfaction and merit of Christ. By His passive obedience Christ took upon Him and bore the penalty of sins, so that they should no longer be imputed to converted or renewed sinners. By His active obedience Christ most perfectly fulfilled the divine law in place of the fallen human race, so that His vicarious fulfilling of the law might be imputed for righteousness to the sinner who believes in Him.

Justification, therefore, consists of two parts, negative, the non-imputation of sin, or their remission, corresponding with the passive obedience; and positive: the imputation of the righteousness of Christ corresponding with the active obedience. These parts though distinguishable are indivisible, each in its fullness involves the other.

The instrumental cause of justification, or receptive medium, is faith. We are justified through faith, but not on account of faith, but on account of Christ. Faith alone justifies not on account of itself, its own dignity or value moving God to justify the believer, but because as an instrument or a receptive medium, it lays, hold of the merit of Christ, in view of which merit, considers the sinner as righteous.

The believer in receiving the imputation Christ's righteousness, also has the elements imparted, the righteousness of a new obedience. Justification is never completed where sanctification has never begun; but the justification must not be conditioned on the sanctification, but the sanctification is in its beginning the invariable result of justification. We are not justified because we are sanctified, but we begin to be sanctified because we are justified. Sanctification is the outstreaming of the perennial spring of justification—a spring is not made by the flow of water from it, but the flow is produced by the spring.

We are justified by faith alone, but the faith which justifies never is alone, as a light, which has no warmth in it would not be sunlight, and yet it is light and not heat, which is the medium of vision.

Justification is absolutely perfect. We do not begin to be justified as in a state which is to grow, but we are justified absolutely, and can never be more thoroughly justified than we are at the first moment.

The true doctrine of justification is the source of the deepest assurance and of the most ardent and earnest piety. All the attempts to weaken the doctrine arise from confused notions or pernicious errors, in regard to the nature of man, or of God, of faith or works, of justification or sanctification. The self-righteousness of man lilts itself against it. But to the soul brought to the real consciousness of what itself is and what God is, it is a doctrine which testifies to its divine origin by its internal power, and he who has been justified by faith finds that the reality solves every difficulty and dispels every illusion.

Special Definitions of our Dogmaticians.
(1) Definition of Justification.
Quenstedt: "Justification is the external, judicial, gracious act of the most Holy Trinity, by which a sinful man, whose sins are forgiven on account of the merit of Christ apprehended by faith, is accounted just, to the praise of God's glorious grace and justice and to the salvation of the justified."
(2) We are Justified by Faith.
Baier: "For with and through faith man is at once justified; so that the act by which faith is conferred upon man, and the act by which man is justified, are simultaneous, although faith is by nature first in order and justification subsequent to it."
(3) Justification has a Forensic Sense.
Baier: "Justification has a forensic sense, and denotes that act by which God, the judge, pro-nounces righteous the sinner responsible for guilt and liable to punishment, but who believes in Jesus.
Although the Latin word *iustificare* is compounded of the adjective *iustus* and the verb *facere*, it does not denote in general usage, and especially in the Scriptures when sinful man is said to be justified before God, the infusion of an habitual righteousness, but, according to the import of the Hebrew word *hits-dik* (2 Sam. 15: 4; Deut. 25: 1), and the word *dikaioun* in the Septuagint and Paul (Rom. 3 and 4), the Latin *iustificare* is also transferred from an outward to a spiritual court at which men are placed as before a divine tribunal, and are acquitted after the case has been beard and sentence bas been pronounced."
Gerhard: "The forensic signification of the word *dikaioun*, to justify is proved;
"1. Because it denotes a judicial act, not only without reference to the doctrine of gratuitous justification before God (Is. 5: 23; Deut. 25: 1; 2 Sam. 15: 4; Ps. 82: 3; Is. 43: 9), but also in the very article of justification (Ps. 143: 2; Job 9: 2, 3; Luke 18: 14);

"2. Because it is opposed to condemnation (Deut. 25: 1; 1 Kings 8: 32; Prov. 17: 15; Matt. 12: 37; Rom. 5: 16; 8: 33, 34);

"3. Because its correlatives are judicial. For a judgment is mentioned, Ps. 143: 2; a judge, John 5: 27; a tribunal, Rom. 14: 10; a criminal, Rom. 3: 19; a plaintiff, John 5: 45; a witness, Rom. 2: 15; an indictment, Col. 2: 14; an obligation, Matt. 18: 24; an advocate, 1 John 2:1; an acquittal, Ps. 32: 1.

"4. Because the equivalent phrases are judicial. Paul explains justification by a 'reckoning for righteousness', Rom. 4: 3, 5; by 'covering iniquities'; by 'not imputing sin'; by 'forgiving trespasses', Col. 2: 13."

(4) Justification Does Not Mean a Real and Internal Change of Man. Hollaz: "Since justification is a judicial act...and takes place apart from man in God, it cannot intrinsically change man. The point from which this internal change takes place is the state of being responsible for guilt and liable to punishment (Rom. 4: 7; Eph. 1: 7; 2 Cor. 5: 19)...The point to which it conducts is the state of grace and righteousness; because God, remitting the offenses of the sinner who believes in Christ receives him into favor, and imputes to him the righteousness of Christ (Rom. 4: 5, 6; Gal. 3: 6; 2 Cor. 5: 21; Phil. 3: 9; Rom. 5: 19)."

(5) Our Justification Consists of Two Things.
Quenstedt: "Our justification before consists in the remission and non-imputation of sins the imputation of the righteousness of Christ."

Baier: "It is certain, when we call the form justification the forgiveness or non-imputation of sins, the imputation of the righteousness of Christ is not excluded, nor the imputation of this faith itself for righteousness. The imputation of the righteousness of Christ, and of faith itself, is only logically prior to the forensic act of justification by which men are absolved from the guilt of sins."

Quenstedt: "These two parts are not different or distinct essentially (so to speak), but merely logically; for the imputation of Christ's righteousness is essentially nothing else than the remission of sins, and the remission of sins is nothing else than the imputation of Christ's righteousness, so that either word separately taken expresses the whole nature of justification. Whence the Apostle Paul, Rom. 4, interchanges the forgiveness of sins and the imputation of righteousness in his description of justification, which he sometimes defines as the forgiveness of sins, and sometimes as the imputation of righteousness."

Hollaz: "Remission of sins and the imputation of Christ's righteousness are inseparable and closely united acts; but distinct, indeed, in form, as the first is privitive, and the other positive, and as the one results immediately from the passive obedience of Christ, and the other from his active obedience. We do not deny, meanwhile, that the one may probably be inferred from the other, for there is no sinner, whose sins are pardoned, but has the righteousness of Christ imputed, and the reverse."

(6) In What the Form of Imputation Consists.

Quenstedt: "The form of imputation consists in the gracious reckoning of God, by which the penitent sinner, on account of the most perfect obedience oi another, i.e. of Christ, apprehended by faith according to Gospel mercy, is pronounced righteous before the divine tribunal, just as if this obedience had been rendered by the man himself."

Hollaz "Imputation, in the doctrine of justification, is not taken in a physical sense, so as to signify to insert, to implant, but in a moral, judicial, and declarative sense, so as to signify to abjudicate, to attribute, to ascribe, to transfer, confer, devolve upon another the effect of a voluntary act by one's own estimate and decision."

(7) The Reality of This Imputation.

Baier: "It is called imputation, not as an empty or imaginary transfer of the merit of one to another destitute alike of a basis and fruit; but because it is an act of the intellect and will of him who exercises the judgment, by which he adjudges that the merit of one, which is offered for another, and is apprehended by the faith of him for whose benefit it has been offered, can be legitimately accepted as if it were his own merit, and is willing to receive it in such manner as if he had of himself offered it, whatever it is. Paul himself uses this argument in Rom. 4: 3-6."

Quenstedt: "This imputation is most real, whether respect is had to the righteousness which is imputed, or to the act of imputation. The righteousness of Christ, or His obedience, active and passive, which is imputed to us, is most-true and real; for it corresponds entirely to the mind and will of God expressed in the law. The act of imputation, also, or the imputation itself, is real; because its measure is the infallible intellect of God. They, therefore, to whom the righteousness of Christ is imputed, are truly righteous, though not inherently, or by inherence, but imputatively...He is truly just who, in the judgment of God, is regarded as just."

(8) The Ground of Justification is Exterior to Man.
Quenstedt: "The internal cause of our justification is the purely gratuitous grace of God (Rom. 3: 24; 11: 6; Eph. 2: 8, 9; 2 Tim. 1: 9; Tit. 3: 4-6),

"and the external., and meritorious cause is Christ the Mediator, by virtue of His active and passive· obedience (Rom. 3: 24; 2 Cor. 5: 21)."... "This imputation has a most firm foundation, not in man, who is justified, but outside of him, namely, in God Himself, who imputes and in Christ the Mediator, who earned the imputation by rendering satisfaction."

(9) Faith is Only the Subordinate or an Instrumental Cause of Justification, Organic and Receptive.

Hollaz: "The receptive means, or that on the part of the sinner which receives Christ's merit, and the grace of God founded upon it, is faith...Faith justifies not by itself, by its own dignity of value, by moving God to justify the believer, but because, as an instrument or receptive means, it lays hold of the merit of Christ, in view of which and without the least detriment to His justice, God of His mere grace, is moved to pardon and consider righteous the penitent sinner believing in Christ (John 1: 12; Rom. 5: 17; Gal. 3: 14; Acts 10: 43). Faith receives the effects of Christ's satisfaction, the remission of sins. From the sacred oracles we gather that faith is the receptive means by which the satisfaction of Christ, and the grace of God obtained by it, are received."

(10) Justification Differs From New Obedience.
The imputed righteousness of faith is immediately accompanied by an incipient righteousness of new obedience. Ent these two things are not to be confounded or intermingled in the doctrine of justification by faith in the sight of God.

Chemnitz: "It is certain that the blessing bestowed through the Son of God is two-fold, namely, forgiveness of sins and renovation, in which the Holy Spirit enkindles new virtues in believers. For Christ by His passion merited for us not only the remission of sins, but, in addition, this also, that on account of His merit, the Holy Spirit is given to ns that we may be renewed in the spirit of our mind. These benefits of the Son of God, we say, are so united, that when we are reconciled, at the same time the spirit of renovation is also given us. But we do not on this account confound them, but distinguish them, so as to give to each its place, order, and character; as Scripture teaches us, that reconciliation and remission of sins goes before, and that the beginning of love or new obedience follows, and especially that faith concludes that it has a reconciled God and the forgiveness of sins, not on account of the subsequent and commenced renovation (or good works), but on account of the Son God, the Mediator."

(11) We are Justified Before God, and Alone. Melanchthon: "As it is of much importance that this exclusive particle, gratis, by faith alone, without works, should be properly understood, I will explain the. four reasons on account of which it is necessary to retain and defend it:

"(1) That due honor be ascribed to Christ;

"(2) That conscience may maintain a sure and firm consolation;

"(3) That true prayer may be offered;

"(4) That the difference between the Law and the Gospel may be seen."

Chemnitz "Should the inquiry be made why we contend so strenuously for the particle alone, and are not rather contented with those exclusive particles which are contained in the Scriptures, as by grace, freely, without works, the reasons are weighty and true. In the article of justification, we give a prominent place to the exclusive particles of Paul. This particle alone embraces at once, and that very significantly, all the exclusive particles which the Scriptures use.

The Effects of Justification.
Quenstedt: "(1) Our mystical union with God, John 15: 4-6; 14: 23; Gal. 2: 18, 20; 3: 27; Eph. 3: 17;

"(2) Adoption as sons of God, John 1: 12; Rom. 8: 14;

"(3) Peace of conscience, Rom. 5: 1;

"(4) Certain hearing of prayer, Rom.. 8: 32; James 1: 5-7;

"(5) Sanctification, Rom. 6: 12;

"(6) Eternal salvation, Rom. 4: 7, 8."

Properties of Justification.

Quenstedt: "(1) "Immediate efficacy, for it is not gradual and successive, as renovation, but in a moment, an instant, simultaneously and at once.

"(2) Perfection, because all sins are perfectly pardoned, so that there is need of no satisfaction of our own" 1 John 1: 7; Rom. 8: 1; Heb. 10: 14.

"(3) Identity in the mode of justification, in respect to all that are to be saved, Acts 4: 12; 15: 11; Rom. 3: 22-26.

"(4) Assurance in us, not conjectural, but infallible and divine, Rom. 8: 25, 38, 39; 5: 1, 2; Eph. 3: 12; 1 John 3: 14.

"(5) Growth, not as to the act which is simultaneous, but in regard to faith and the consciousness of justification, 2 Cor. 10: 15; Col. 1: 10; 2 Pet. 3: 18; Eph. 4:14, 15.

"(6) Constant continuance. For as the forgiveness of sins, so also our justification is renewed daily, and not only in the first beginning, but faith daily is imputed to the believer for righteousness, and thus our justification is continuous, Rev. 22: 11.

"(7) Amissibility, Heb. 6: 5, 6; John 15: 2.

"(8) Recoverableness, John 6: 37; Rom. 5: 20. The prodigal son is an example, Luke 15."

IX. THE MYSTICAL UNION AND ADOPTION.

In regeneration, in its narrow sense, a man receives faith, and by faith is justified, and then only he begin to be mystically united to God and is adopted as His son, and this mystical union is succeeded by renovation and sanctification. But these acts of grace so cohere that they cannot be separated or rent asunder.

In and with faith and justification, the Holy Spirit becomes the principle of a new life and the bond of a real internal fellowship of life with the triune God continues in the mystical union. This new life of faith appears as a life of eternal fellowship with Christ. To be a Christian is to be in Christ. Christ lives in us.

The Spirit of Christ is in us. We are led by the Spirit; our members are the body of Christ; we are partakers of the divine nature; we are partakers in the moral characteristics, love and holiness of Christ. The Father and the Son and the Holy Ghost make their abode in the believer. He abides in God and God in him.

That faith which justifies also renews, and the Holy Ghost who is given through the Word and the Sacraments to make us believers, is in that same divine act given to us to make us saints. Believers and saints are the same persons. No one can be a believer without, as the necessary and immediate consequence, becoming a saint. No man can be a saint without being a believer. The Holy Spirit comes to us in order to our faith and dwells in us when we believe. It is not God's gift apart from God which dwells in us; but God's gifts come to us with God and they dwell in us because God dwells in us. The saint is the temple of the Trinity, not, however, the mere locality of their presence but knit to them by the bond of the mystical union, and the believer is also adopted as the son of God.

Some of our dogmaticians in this place of the dogmatic system discuss Regeneration in its broader sense which has already been discussed under the beading Regeneration in its narrow sense.

The Scripture Doctrine of the Mystical Union.

The Mystical Union.

The mystical union, as the result of indwelling grace, is the spiritual conjunction of the triune God with the justified man in whom as a temple hallowed to Himself God dwells by special personal presence, not the presence of separated gilts but of substance bringing the gifts and operating by a gracious influence in him. As a part of this mystical union, there is a conjunction, true and real, and most close, of the divine-human nature of Christ, the God-man with the renewed man. This conjunction takes place by virtue of the merit of Christ through the Word and Sacraments, so that Christ constitutes, as it were, one spirit with the renewed man and works in him and through him and appropriates or treats, as his own, these things which the believer does or suffers, so that the man, as to his divine life no longer lives of himself, but in the faith of the Son of God until he reaches the heavenly life.

It is a mystery of the deepest kind that God the infinite dwells in the human heart and perfects His work there through His indwelling spirit in a supernatural mode.

The means on the part of God are the Word God and the Sacraments; In the part of man, faith.

The pure doctrine of the mystery is opposed two extremes,

(1) That of the false mysticism which obliterates the boundary between God and man and teaches a fellowship, of essence;

(2) It is also opposed to the rationalistic prosy conception which separates the benefits conferred by God from His personal indwelling.

Adoption.

When we are justified by faith, we are not only united to Christ, but we are also adopted as sons of God, Gal. 3: 26; 4: 5, 6. As long as we still did not believe in Christ, we were bond servants under the law, Gal. 3: 23; 4: 1, 3, and as slaves we had no part in the inheritance, Gal. 4: 7. But by justifying faith we passed from a state of slavery to a state of sonship, Gal. 3: 25, 26. To be under the influence of the spirit of God is an evidence of divine sonship, Rom.

8: 14, and we receive the spirit of adoption, whereby we cry, Abba, Father, Rom. 8: 15, and being sons we are heirs, joint-heirs with Christ, 8: 17, and as such have a title to our inheritance, Gal. 4: 7. The Father's love now rests upon the believer, and he can have the trust and confidence of a child, Gal. 4: 6.

The divine sonship of Paul is the same as the "children of God" those "begotten of God," of which John speaks in John 1: 12 and in 1 John 3: 9, 10; 5: 1, 2.

There are certain special privileges which belong to believers as adopted sons of God. Scripture especially mentions 1) freedom from a servile fear, Rom. 8: 15; Gal. 4: 7; 1John 4: 18; 2) the being the objects of the Father's peculiar love, Rom. 5: 9-11; 1 John 3: 1; 3) the guidance and indwelling of the Holy Ghost, Rom. 8: 14; Gal. 4: 5, 6; 4) a child-like confidence in God, Gal. 4: 6; Rom. 8: 15; and 5) the certain inheritance of the riches of our Father's glory, as heirs of God, and joint-heirs with Christ, 1 Cor. 3: 21-23; Gal. 4: 7; Rom. 8: 17.

The Greek word for adoption (*uiothesia*) is not used by any of the New Testament writers, although both Jesus Himself and all speak frequently and emphatically of our blessings and duties as sons or children of God, save by St. Paul alone, who used it in five places (Gal. 4: 5; Rom. 8: 15, 23; 9: 4; Eph. 1: 5).

The earliest instance of the use of the word is in Gal. 4: 5, in a passage in which several names of human relations are used to illustrate those used between God and man. The blessing brought by Christ in the fullness of time is called adoption, and this seems to indicate that St. Paul holds the sonship, of which he is speaking, to be founded on the covenant promise of God, and not on the natural relation of God to all men as such. It is a position bestowed by a disposition of God, and through redemption by Christ. It gives not merely paternal care, but the complete rights of sonship, the gift of the Spirit of God's Son and the inheritance. It is founded upon a spiritual union to God's Son, which is described as putting on Christ, Gal. 3: 27. Some theologians have inferred from the connection between redemption and adoption, in this passage, that adoption is the positive part of the complete blessing of justification, of which forgiveness is the negative part. But there is a difference between the two that evidently St. Paul meant by adoption a blessing distinct from our having peace with God and access into His favor, which he describes in Rom. 5: 1 as the positive fruits of our justification.

The next place where St. Paul speaks of adoption is in Rom. 8: 15, 23. The line of reasoning is the same as in Galatians but put in the inverse order. The promise of life is proved by the fact of our being sons of God; and that again, because the spirit that He has given us is that of adoption, enabling us to address God as our Father, and so witnessing with our spirit that we are children of God, and stating that this adoption carries with it all the rights of true sonship (8: 16, 17). So in 8: 23 he says: "We wait for our adoption, the redemption of our body." It is the resurrection of life at the coming of the Lord that is undoubtedly meant; and that is called here the adoption, because it will be the full revelation of our sonship. Now are we the sons of God as St. John puts it; but the world knoweth us not and it doth not yet appear what we shall be; but when it shall appear we shall be like Him (1 John 3: 1-3).

In Rom. 9: 4, St. Paul mentions the adoption first among the privileges of Israel, which he there enumerates. He implies that they had this relation, not through physical descent or creation, but by an act of gracious love on God's part. And in 9: 7, 8, St, Paul teaches that not all the children of Abraham and Jacob are children of God but they who are of the promise, i.e. they who accept the promise by faith.

The last place that St. Paul uses the term is Eph. 1: 5, where he says that God eternally predestinated believers unto adoption as sons through Jesus Christ unto Himself. This refers to the eternal purpose and corresponds to what he had said in Rom. 8: 29 that "whom He did foreknow, He also did predestinate to be conformed to the likeness of His Son, that He might be the first born among many brethren." The grace of adoption makes believers truly Christ's brethren and joint heirs with Him.

The Church Doctrine.
Time of the Mystical Union.
Quenstedt: "Regeneration, justification, union, and renovation, are simultaneous, and in being more closely united than the ingredients of an atom, so cohere that it cannot be separated or rent asunder. Yet to our mode of conceiving of them...regeneration precedes, that faith may be attained; justification follows, which is

of faith; the mystical union then occurs, which is succeeded by renovation and sanctification."

Definition of Mystical Union.
Quenstedt: "The mystical union is the real and most intimate conjunction of the substance of the Holy Trinity and the God-man Christ with the substance of believers, affected by God Himself through the Gospel, the sacraments, and faith, by which, through a special approximation of His essence, and by a gracious operation, He is in them, just as also believers are in Him; that, by a mutual and reciprocal immanence they may partake of His vivifying power and all His mercies, become assured of the grace of God and eternal salvation, and preserve unity in the faith, and love with the members of His mystical body."

Proof of the Mystical Union.
Quenstedt: "The mystical union is provided:
"(1) From the promise of Christ, John 14: 23, 15: 26;
"(2) From the indwelling in believers, Eph. 3: Rom. 8: 9; 2 Cor. 6: 16;
"(3) From the unity of believers with God, 17: 21;
"(4) From the partaking of the divine nature."

Difference Between a General Union With God and This Special Mystical Union.
Quenstedt: "The general union of all men with the substance of God the Creator is indicated in Acts 17: 28, where the preposition in expresses the general presence of God with men."
Hollaz: "The special mystical union is partly a gracious one in the Church Militant, whereby God dwells in the regenerate by His substantial presence, and operates in them by His special concurrence, John 14: 23; 17: 11, 21; and partly a glorious one, in the triumphant assembly of the elect, whereby God fills and delights the elect with the plentitude of His grace, 1 Cor. 15: 28,"

This Mystical Union is not a Substantial One.
Hollaz: "(1) God dwells in us as in temples, by the favor of the mystical union, 1 Cor. 3: 16; but the habitation is not changed into the inhabitant, nor the inhabitant into the habitation;

"(2) By the mystical union we put on Christ, Gal. 3: 27; but the garment is not essentially one with the person who wears it;

"(3) The divine nature is very distinct from the human, although God comes to us and makes His abode with us, John 14: 23, but He can depart from man to whom He has come. The mystical union is, indeed, called a union of substances, but, strictly taken, not a formal substantial union...but it is an accidental union."

This Mystical Union is not a Personal Union.
Quenstedt: "The mystical union does not consist in a personal union or a coalition of extremes united into one hypostasis or person, such as is the union of the divine and human nature in Christ; so that the believer, united to Christ, could say, I am Christ."

Hollaz: "Paul teaches that Christ and believers being mystically united remain distinct persons, Gal. 2: 20."

X. RENOVATION, SANCTIFICATION AND GOOD WORKS.

The new life in the believer manifests and unfolds itself in the life of love which pertains to sanctification. This is the result of the co-working of the activity of God and man. It gives evidence of its reality in a constant warfare against sin (renovation) and in the constant growth toward fellowship with God. It reveals itself in good works, and is completed in the glorification of the life to come, in the image of Christ.

Scripture Doctrine.
All the apostolic exhortations to holiness rest on the supposition that those to whom it is addressed are already possessed of salvation.

Sanctification is that in which the Christian shows what he has become through the grace of God. We are created anew in Jesus Christ unto good works which God has before ordained that we should walk in them.

The manifestation of the new life is negative and positive. It is negative in denying sin, in putting off the old man with his deeds, renouncing with the flesh, the world and the devil (Col. 3; 9; Eph. 4: 22); it is positive in putting on the new man, which is renewed unto full knowledge according to the image of Him that created him (Col. 3: 10; Eph. 4: 24), growing in Christ, advancing in good works, adding virtue to virtue. Sanctification reaches everything whatsoever we do in word or deed. The essence of the new life is love to God and to God's children, and to our neighbor though he be not God's child. It is in antithesis to selfishness. It is the true fulfilling of the law. It forms a necessary presupposition to our fellowship with Christ in the eternal world. Without it no man shall see the Lord. Its degrees form the measure of reward in eternity. As we sow here, we reap in heaven. Our labor is not in vain in the Lord, and our works do follow us.

Church Doctrine.

The Early Church.

The early mingling which took place between the conceptions of justification and sanctification arose from the legal tendency, which every system, including Judaism, had stamped upon the thinking of our race. The merit of good works is connected at once with what is deepest in man's moral aspirations and with his most inordinate self-estimation. To do good works which God would esteem as such is something for which a good man would intensely yearn, and which a vain man would be most tempted to think he had attained.

Augustine had derived from his bitter experience of the corruption of his nature, the preparation for the gospel doctrine, the inability of man lo all meritorious works. He saw that man's great need was to be delivered from the bondage of the law by the guidance of the spirit. But the whole church of the West more and more perverted the gospel into legalism and with the idea of merit. Just in proportion, as men have a shallow conception of what holiness is, do they attach value to our own.

The Middle Ages.

In the Middle Ages the doctrine was strictly taught that a man may, by good works, merit heaven. distinction was drawn between obeying the commandments of God and conforming to the evangelical counsels, advice or recommendations in the Gospel. These latter were referred to the voluntary poverty, celibacy, and monastic vows through which it was supposed, a state of perfection could be attained. Everybody is obliged to keep the precepts in moral conformity to the law of God, was therefore, considered a matter of course and little esteemed, while the works of supererogation, those beyond the commands, performed by those who did more than they were com· mantled to do, were highly esteemed.

The self-imposed imaginary duties, poverty, celibacy, were more esteemed than true holiness; and a man often began his more perfect life by abandoning all his natural duties.

The Reformation.

The Reformation did a great work in restoring the true conception and foundation of Christian holiness, in exalting God's law and overthrowing man's tradition, in teaching that no works perfectly fulfill the requirements of God, and that none can transcend it. It leads men to the great divine idea that holiness is an internal condition, that faith is the spring of good works, not by prescription or coercion, but by the law of its nature. The law is indeed needed by believers as the guide of life, the directory in the divine way, the guide book does not force the traveler over the route he abhors, but helps him to pursue the route he desires to take. The law is needed also by believers or the repression of the remnant of in dwelling corruption, not as coercing, but as medicinal and healing. The most perfect saint, relatively is really as much below the absolute standard of God's will, as he is above the standard of the godless man. God's works are to be done, because they are the exercise in which faith strengthens life, because they are the tokens of a regenerate nature, the most effectual form of confessing our Saviour and God, of showing forth our gratitude for His great benefits and approving that we are sharers of His Spirit.

Good works are, relatively to the human standard, meritorious; there is in the character of the good man as such that which God approves and rewards as over against the character of a bad man. Good works are not meritorious relatively to the divine standard. Were they perfect they would only be what is due, and therefore not entitled to reward, but they are imperfect. The unjustified man does not reach justification by works, but passes out of condemnation into justification by faith, but the justified man reaches higher degree of reward as he is faithful in his co-working with God who worketh in Him and there are grades of rewarding both in this world and the world to come.

We are debtors to do good works, we are bound to do them. Good works are necessary, not by coercion as if anything produced by coercion could be precious to God, but by the necessity which inheres in the moral nature of the renewed man. A regenerate man as such cannot but do good works, and a man who does out ward works, seemingly good, only under coercion, is not a regenerate man. They who of the law need no coercion are in bondage under the law, he cannot but strive to fulfill are free from this bondage. They that are in bondage if a man be under grace; the law for this is the impulse of grace. If he be under the law, he is a debtor; unto bonds for its fulfillment. Striving unto holiness, or the way to holiness, is two-fold which may be called renovation, the privative or negative side and sanctification the positive side.

The privative or negative side (renovation) implies the removal of everything evil; the positive (sanctification) implies the presence of everything good. As privative it removes the darkness from the understanding, the aversion from the will. It is not perfect in this life; but advances through warfare and struggles towards that final consummation that awaits it in a better world. The conflict between the flesh and the Spirit never ceases in this life; and he who is deepest in the divine life is most removed from the temptation to claim perfection with it. As positive it gives the ampler illumination of the mind; purification of the desires, heavenly energies of the will, and in so far as it does these things it restores the divine image.

The development of christian character must be carried on by a continual dying unto sin, and a continual rising again to newness of life (Rom. 6: 4-11), a progressive realization of personal growth and holiness. Both processes must be combined in order to true christian development and no work deserves the name of Christian which is not on the one hand a purifying and renovating work, whose aim is to banish the power of sin, and on the other hand, a holy and creative work, which accomplishes a new thing upon earth.

The Teaching of our Dogmaticians.
Renovation is the Negative, Sanctification the Positive. Schmid: "God desires that the justified man should cease to be the old man, and become a new man, leading day by day a more holy life before God. And God Himself works in this direction by His divine grace, seeking to draw off man more and more from sin, and to encourage and strengthen him for that which is good.

This operation, wrought by God in man, is called renovation, so far as through it a change is wrought in man, in consequence of which he may be called a new man; it is called sanctification so far as now his life begins to become holy."

Full Definition Including Renovation and Sanctification.

Hollaz: "Renovation is an act of grace, whereby the Holy Spirit, expelling the faults of a justified man endows him with inherent sanctity. The change that takes place in man consists further in this, that by the influence of divine grace the sin still cleaving to man disappears, more and more, and gives place to an increasing facility for doing what is good. As the sinfulness yet remaining in man yields only through a constantly repeated struggle against sin, this renovation is not a sudden, but a gradual one, susceptible of constant growth; and as sin never entirely leaves man, it is never perfect, although we are always to strive after perfection. Finally, it is a work of God in man, yet of such a nature that there is a free co-operation on the part of man, who has received new spiritual powers."

Renovation Differs from Regeneration and Justification.
Quenstedt: "Renovation differs 1) as to the efficient cause. Regeneration and justification are actions of God alone: renovation is indeed an action of God, but not of God alone, for the regenerate man also concurs, not in his own strength, but through divinely granted power.

2) As to the subject. Man altogether dead in sins is the subject of regeneration. The sinner indeed is the subject of justification, Rom. 4: 5, 17, yet one recognizing his sins and believing in Christ; but the subject of renovation is man already justified.

3) As to the object. Regeneration is occupied with the production of faith; justification with imputed righteousness; renovation with inherent righteousness.

4) As to the form. Regeneration consists in the bestowment of spiritual life, and a transfer from a state of wrath to a state of grace; justification in the remission of sins and the imputation of Christ's righteousness; but renovation in the reformation of the mind, will, and affections, and so of the whole man, or in the restoration of the divine image, commenced in this life and to be completed in the next.

5) As to the properties. Both regeneration and justification are instantaneous; renovation is progressive, from day to day.

6) As to the order. Regeneration precedes justification, and justification precedes renovation. Renovation is related to justification as an effect to a cause, and follows it, not in the order

of time, hut of nature. There- fore Paul does not use these words indiscriminately, Tit. 3: 5."

The Starting-Point and Goal of Renovation.

Quenstedt: "The old man is the starting- point, the new man the goal, Eph. 4: 22; Col. 3:10"

Hollaz: "The remains of sin are the starting-point of renovation...and are to be abolished by daily renovation that they may be diminished and suppressed. The point to which renovation tends is a more clear and comprehensive understanding or knowledge of spiritual things, inherent righteousness and holiness in the will...a restoration of the divine image."

The Form of Renovation.

Hollaz: "The form of renovation consists in the expulsion of mental errors and the illumination of the mind, Col. 3: 10; Rom. 12: 2; in the rectification of the will and the renewing of righteousness and true holiness, Eph. 4: 24; in the restraining of the appetites inclined to evil; in the purity and chastity of the affections; in the employment of the members of the body in works of righteousness, Rom. 12: 1; in the subduing of the dominion of sin, Rom. 6: 13, 19."

Renovation and Sanctification are Progressive.

Hollaz: "As the body of sin in process of time is more and more weakened by the regenerate man, so the regenerate man is transformed more and more into the image of God from glory to glory by the Holy Spirit. 2 Cor. 3: 18; 4: 16.

Renovation and Sanctification Admit of Degrees.

Quenstedt: "For sin remains in the regenerate, affects their self-control; the flesh lusts against the Spirit, and therefore our renovation progresses from day to day and is to be continued through life, 2 Cor. 4: 16...Renovation is increased by godly acts and frequent efforts. These being intermitted or diminished...so there is at one time an increase in sanctification, at another a decrease. The Holy Scriptures expressly affirm that the renovation of the regenerate in this life ought continually to increase and grow, Eph. 4: 16."

The Efficient Cause of Sanctification.

Quen: "The first efficient cause is the entire Trinity (1 Thess. 5: 23: John 15: 4, 5), terminatively and appropriately, the Holy Spirit (Rom. 15: 16; Tit. 3: 5; Rom. 1: 4; Gal. 5: 22)."

Hollaz: "Sanctification is, indeed, common to all three persons of the godhead, and accordingly is ascribed to God the Father, John 17: 17, and God the Son, Heb. 9: 14. But in the Holy Scriptures and the Apostles Creed the Holy Spirit is characterized by an outward work of discrimination, as it were, so that He is said to sanctify us, terminatively, Rom. 15: 16.

The Regenerate Man Cooperates with God in the Work of Sanctification.
Hollaz: "The regenerate and justified man concurs in the work of sanctification, not by an equal action, but in subordination and dependence on the Holy Spirit, because he works, not with native but with granted powers. This is inferred from the words of the Apostle, Phil. 2: 12, 13."

Definition of Good Works.
Hollaz: "Good works are free acts of justified persons, performed through the renewing grace of the Holy Spirit, according to the prescription of the divine law, through faith in Christ preceding, to the honor of God and the edification of men...By works here are understood not only external visible actions, such as precede from the hand or tongue, but internal affections of the heart and movements of the will, and thus the entire obedience and inherent righteousness of the regenerate. Internal good works are seen by the eyes of God alone, and comprise the inner thoughts of the mind, the movements of the will, and the pure affection of the heart, such as love, the fear of God, confidence toward God, patience, humility. The external good works are seen not only by God, but likewise by man, and manifest themselves by outward demeanor words, and actions...A good intention is to be accounted among good internal works."

Why the Works of Justified Men are Called Good.
Hollaz: "The works of regenerate and justified mon are called good, not absolutely, as if they were perfectly good, but in their kind, because 1) they derive their origin from the good Spirit of God, Ps. 143: 10;

2) they proceed from a good heart, Matt. 12: 35; 3) they are in some degree conformed to the good will of God, expressed in the law, Rom. 12: 2; and 4) they design good end, the glory of God."

Yet all Good Works are Imperfect.
Hollaz: "The good works of regenerated and renovated men do not reach that degree of perfection that they cannot increase, Eph. 4: 15, nor do they perfectly correspond to the divine law, Rom. 7:14, nor are they so complete that they can sustain the rigid scrutiny of di- vine justice, Ps. 143: 2, but they are still imperfect, James 3, 2."

Their Source is True and Living Faith in Christ.
Hollaz: "The source through which the renewed man performs good works is true and living faith in Christ, Gal. 5: 6, which is called the cause of good works by emanation, Matt. 5: 16."

The Upright Works of Unregenerate Men Cannot be Called Good.
Hollaz: "The upright works of unregenerate men, whether they be out of the church or have an external connection with it, which contribute to external order and the preservation of society, are civilly and morally to some extent good; but they are not good theologically and spiritually, nor do they please God; and, therefore, in as much as they are destitute of the constituents of really good works, they are properly called splendid sins.

Characterization of Spiritually Good Work.
Apology: "1) They are the fruits of the Spirit, Gal. 5: 22; 2) They are performed by persons reconciled to God through Christ: 3) They proceed from a pure heart, a good conscience, and faith unfeigned, 1 Tim. 1: 5; 4) They are spontaneous and free actions; 5) They are directed to the glory of God.

Good Works Should not be Constrained but be Spontaneous and Free.
Quen: "They are necessary, neither to acquire salvation (as a means), nor to earn salvation (as a merit), nor to obtain salvation (as an indispensable condition or cause), nor to reach it (as a mode of coming to a final goal), nor finally, to preserve it (as a conserving cause). But we hold good works to be necessary, by the necessity, 1) of the divine command, Mal. 1: 6; Matt, 5: 44; 2) of our duty, or of gratitude due for the benefits of creation, redemption, etc. 3) of

presence, that believers may not lose the grace of God and faith, and fall from the hope of the inheritance; 4) of a divinely appointed order and sequence to justification and faith, because as effects they necessarily follow their cause."

Good Works have their Reward.
Hollaz: "The regenerate have respect in the performance of Good works: 1) to the glory of God, (1 Cor. 10: 31; 2) they may have respect with filial affection to the remunerations of this and a future life, not as due reward or master's compensation, but as gratuitous gifts and divine blessings, to terminate ultimately in the Glory of God, 1 Tim. 4:8."

The Christian Warfare.
Quen: Definition, "The performance of good works in its widest extent can be called the christian warfare. For the life of the faithful christian this continual spiritual warfare is a daily contest, and an eternal enmity to everything which is opposed to the will of God and His kingdom, 1 Tim. 1: 18; 2 Tim 2: 3. He fights by faith, hope and patience.

Enemies: The enemies against whom he must fight are the devil, the world, and the flesh.

Arms: The arms of the spiritual warfare are described, 2 Cor. 10: 4-6; Eph. 6: 10-17; 1 Peter 5: 8, 9.

Standard: The standard under which we fight is the banner of the cross, Matt. 16: 24."

CLOSING SUMMARY

We have traced the founding of the fellowship of God in His eternal will of love. We have seen man created and placed in the world as the beginning of the historical actualizing of the divine will of love; we have contemplated God in His creation and providence as the author of miracles, the sovereign of angels, even of the fallen angels; the father of man in man's original state and in the fall; we have seen the disturbance of the original fellowship of God by sin and the preparation for its restoration, delivery of man from the power of original sin and of transgression.

We have seen how this fellowship was restored in Christ Jesus, how this fellowship is actually applied to us and appropriated by us personally; by the grace of the Holy spirit we are called, enlightened, regenerated, and converted; through true penitence for sin we are prepared in faith to lay hold of the merit in Christ Jesus and are justified, and thus our life and fellowship with God is consummated. We are adopted in the family of God as dear children are, in the fellowship of life with Christ, in the mysterious but not most real union with the adorable Trinity, and are co-workers with our God in bringing forth those Holy works which are in keeping with His nature and will, and which are the tokens of a renewed and sanctified heart.

SELECT LITERATURE OF PNEUMATOLOGY.

We do not aim to give a complete bibliography. We have only selected the most important works that may be helpful to the student.

BAIER, Compendium Theol. Positivae, (Walther) 1879.
BESTE, Martin Luthers GlaubenSlehre. 1845.
BIRKS, Justification and Imputed Righteousness. 1887. Book of Concord. (Lutheran Confession).
BUCHANAN, The Office and Work of the Holy Spirit. 1847.
BUCHANAN, The Doctrine of Justification. 1867.
CANDLISH, The Work of the Holy Spirit.
CREMER, Biblical Theological Lexicon of New Testament Greek. 1880
DORNER, System of Christian Doctrine. (4 vols.) 1880.

Early Fathers.
ANTI-NICENE FATHERS, (10 vol.)
NICENE and POST-NICENE FATHERS, 1st series. (14 vols.)
NICENE and POST-NICENE FATHERS, 2nd series, (14 vols.)

EWER, The Operation of the Holy Spirit. 1880.
FRANK, System der Christ Wahrheit. (3rd edition) 1894.
GERHARD, Loci Theologici. (9 vols.)
HAGEN BACH, History of Doctrines. (Smith, 2 vols.)
HASE, Hutterus Redivivus, (12th edition) 1883.
HOLLAZ, Evang. Gnadenordnung. 1893.
KOESTLIN, Theology of Luther. (Hay., 2 vols.)
KOESTLIN, Der Glaube.
KRAUTH, Conservative Reformation and its Theology. 1872.
KUYPER, The Work of the Holy Spirit. 1900,
LOY, Doctrine of Justification. 1869.
LUTHARDT Compendium der Dogmatik. (9th edition).
LUTHARDT, Saving Truths of Christianity. 1868.
MARTENSEN, Christian Dogmatics. 1866.
MASON, The Faith of the Gospel. 1894.
MONLE, Outlines of Christian Doctrine. 1902.

VAN OOSTERZEE. Christion Dogmatics. (2 vols.) 1874.

PHILIPPI, Kirch. Glaubenslehre. (9 vols.)

New Schaff-Herzog Encyclopedia. (12 vols.)

SCHMID, Doc. Theol. of Evangel. Luth. Church.

SEEBERG, History of Doctrines. (Hay., 2 vols.)

SMEATON, The Doctrine of the Holy Spirit. 1882.

STRONG, Systematic Theology. (3 vols.) 1907.

VAUGHAN, The Gill of the Holy Spirit. 1900.

VILMAR, Dogmatik. (2 vols.) 1874.

WEIDNER, Christian Ethics. 1891.

WUTTKE, Sittenlehre. (2nd edition) 1865.

ZEZSCHWITZ, Die Christenlehre im Zusammenhang. (3 vols.) 1883.

EXAMINATION QUESTIONS ON PNEUMATOLOGY.

Introduction.
1. As review, how may the subject of Dogmatics be divided?
2. What topics will be discussed under Pneumatology?

THE PERSONAL APPROPRIATION OF SALVATION.
3. Under what two general heads may the Appropriation of the Fellowship of God be discussed?
4. What may be said of the arrangement of the material?
5. What does Hollaz say of the Order of Grace?
6. In what sense does he use the word Regeneration?

I. THE GRACE OF THE HOLY SPIRIT.
I. The Scripture Doctrine.
7. Define Grace.
8. How is it manifested?
9. Show that it is the Active Principle in Salvation.
10. To what does Grace stand in antithesis?
11. Show that the Holy Spirit is the applier of salvation.
12. Show that the Holy Spirit is the divine principle of the new life.
2. The Church Doctrine.
13. Distinguish between the teaching of the Greek Church and that of Augustine.
14. How do our older dogmaticians express the relation of grace to the human will and works?
15. How does Luther express it in his Small Catechism?
16. What does the Formula of Concord say?
17. Show that the acts of grace are closely united.
18. How does Hollaz define grace?
3. Later Development.
19. Give Baier's definition of prevenient grace.
20. How does Hollaz define preparing grace?
21. Give the definition of operating grace.
22. Of cooperating grace.
23. Of preserving grace.
24. Of glorifying grace.

25. What does Quenstedt say of assisting and indwelling grace?
26. What are the acts of grace called before conversion, in conversion, and after conversion?
27. What does Quenstedt say of the effects of the working of grace?
28. What is the four-fold office of the Holy Spirit?
29. Discuss Mysticism.
30. Discuss Rationalism and Supernaturalism.

II. CALLING OR VOCATION.
The Scripture Doctrine.
31. Why is the calling the first act of grace?
32. Illustrate by the example of Christ.
33. Illustrate by the teaching of the Apostles.
34. Illustrate in the manner of God's acting in our salvation.
35. Show that the call is earnest and urgent,
36. Show that it is designed for the whole race.
37. Show that it has been gradual.
2. The Church Doctrine.
38. Define the call.
39. How does Luthardt criticize the definition of Hollaz?
40. Define the general, or indirect, call.
41. What does it accomplish?
42. Distinguish between the ordinary and extraordinary direct call.
43. Contrast Lutheranism and Calvinism on the subject of the call.
44. Show that the call is serious.
45. Show that it is efficacious.
46. How does Quenstedt define the form of the call?
47. What does he say of the Calvinistic teaching?
48. Show that the call is universal.
49. What does Quenstedt say?
50. What do our dogmaticians say of the universality of the call?
51. What is the true solution?
52. What remarkable facts are brought out by modern research?
53. What is the testimony of Hollaz?
54. Why are some nations destitute of the gospel?
55. What is our duty?
56. Discuss more fully the whole question.

III. ILLUMINATION.
I. The Scripture Doctrine.

57. How does Scripture represent the natural condition of man?

58. In contrast how is Christ represented?

59. What is the effect of the Divine witness of the Word?

2. The Church Doctrine.

60. What was the tendency of the Greek Church?

61. How did the Greek Fathers designate baptism?

62. When was the topic of Illumination first separately treated?

63. How does Hollaz describe the condition of the unilluminated man?

64. What is the goal of Illumination?

65. What is the design of Illumination?

66. Define Illumination.

67. Show that Illuinination is teaching grace and anointing grace.

68. Show that it is not confined to the regenerate.

69. Show that Illumination is legal and evangelical.

70. Show that the Holy Spirit illuminates us through the Word.

71. Criticize the so-called doctrine of "sensible assurance."

72. Discuss Illumination more fully.

73. Show that our dogmaticians do not bind Illumination to the single personal act of hearing or reading the Word.

74. What was the teaching of the Mystics?

75. In antithesis what did our divines teach?

76. Show that not only the intellect but also the will must be enlightened.

77. Explain John 7: 17.

78. Show that men may be enlightened but not divinely Illumined.

79. Criticize Mysticism.

80. Show that imperfect Illumination is literal and pedagogic.

81. Show that perfect Illumination is spiritual and saving.

82. How does Quenstedt express the distinction?

83. How does Hollaz draw the distinction between imperfect and perfect illumination?

84. Show that imperfect illumination is supernatural as well as the perfect illumination.

85. Show that illumination is a gradual process.

86. How does Hollaz express this?

87. What ls the proximate end of illumination?

88. What is the ultimate end?

89. Discuss the awakening.

90. What does Martensen say of the awakening?

91. What does Thomasius say?
92. How does illumination differ from regeneration?
93. In what does it differ from sanctification?

IV. REGENERATION IN THE NARROW SENSE.
1. The Scripture Doctrine.
94. What names are given in the New Testament to the new birth?
95. In what two-fold sense is the word Regeneration used?
96. Show that it is used in both senses in the New Testament.
97. What is its usage in the Formula of Concord?
98. How is it used by our earlier dogmaticians?
99. What is its strictest usage?
100. How is it used in its widest sense?
101. How do we use it in our discussion?
102. Of how many birthdays of the believer may we speak?
103. In the New Testament what does the pneuma or spirit of man indicate?
104. How does Plummer distinguish between the pneuma or spirit and the psyche or soul?
105. How does Cremer distinguish between them?
106. Show that the Spirit is the principle of life.
107. Illustrate in the case of death.
108. Prove from Scripture that the pneuma is the divine life principle.
109. Explain Rom, 8: 16.
110. Explain Rom. 8: 9.
111. Show that the *pneuma* forms the basis of the communion. of the new creation.
112. Explain Eph. 1: 13.
113. What is the usage in the New Testament of the word soul?
114. Show that spirit and soul are not identical in the New Testament.
115. Explain the meaning of Heb. 4 : 12:
116. Explain 1 Thess. 5 : 23.
2. General Discussion.
117. What was the condition of the spirit and soul of man before the Fall?
118. After the Fall?
119. Describe more fully the condition of the spirit after the Fall.
120. Describe more fully the condition of the soul.

121. Show that in Christ a new beginning was established. Why can Christ give spiritual life to man?

122. Explain 1 Cor. 15: 49.

123. Why is the new birth a new Creation?

124. Show that the point of entrance of the new birth is the conscience of man.

125. Explain more fully this work of the Holy Spirit on the spirit of the mind.

126. What marks Regeneration in its narrow sense?

127. Show that the believer must become a partaker of the spirit, the soul and the body of Christ.

128.

129. How do we become partaker of the spirit of Christ?

130. How do We become partaker of Christ's soul?

131. How do we become partaker of the flesh or body of Christ?

132. How does Delitzsch express this?

133. What do we learn from John. 3: 7, 8?

134. Show that man is absolutely passive in Regeneration.

135. Show that we cannot distinguish the divine agencies in their beginning or in their progress.

136. Show that regeneration, in its narrow sense, takes place in the region of our unconsciousness.

137. Show that the adult can do nothing positively in Regeneration in the narrow sense.

138. Show that it is easier for an infant to be regenerated in the narrow sense, than for an adult.

139. Around what question does the whole subject center?

140. Discuss some false views.

141. What is conscious or discursive faith?

142. What distinction does Brenz make in faith?

143. What kind of faith do infants have, according to Hollaz?

144. Show that infants have direct faith.

145. Show that this distinction of direct and conscious faith is not unknown in the New Testament.

146. Illustrate it in the preaching of the Word.

147. Show that Baptism is not to be repeated.

148. Show that the validity of Baptism does not depend upon the faith of the believer.

149. What does God bestow in the gift of Baptism?

150. Discuss more fully the blessings of direct faith in the case of the infant, and of conscious faith on the part of the adult.

151. Give the testimony of Pontoppidan.

152. Discuss the subject of consciousness in a child.

153. Discuss God's ability to work upon the conscience and inner spiritual life of the child.

3. The Church Doctrine.

154. How does Baier define regeneration?

155. What, according to Quenstedt, is its starting point?

156. What is its goal?

157. How does Hollaz distinguish between regeneration of adults and of children?

158. How does Chemnitz explain the faith of infants?

159. How does Krauth explain the receptive faith of an infant?

160. How does Hollaz define the form of regeneration?

161. Show that regeneration does not destroy nature.

162. Show that regeneration is a new creation.

163. Show that the regeneration of infants is instantaneous.

164. Show that the ordinary regeneration of adults is successive.

165. Show that regeneration on the part of God is perfect.

166. Show that on the part of man receiving it, it is imperfect.

167. Show that regeneration can be resisted.

168. How does Quenstedt state this?

169. Show that regeneration in the wide sense may be lost.

170. Show that regeneration in the narrow sense always remains alive.

171. State the difference between regeneration and conversion.

V. CONVERSION.

I. Usage of the Word.

172. What is subjective conversion?

173. In what four-fold sense is the word used?

174. Distinguish between transitive and intransitive Conversion.

175. In what sense do we here use the word?

2. The Scripture Doctrine.

176. How is the word to convert used in the New Testament?

177. Show that conversion is sometimes referred to God as the absolute Cause.

178. Show that it is sometimes referred to the minister of God as the instrumental cause.

179. Show that it is sometimes referred to man as a moral agent.
     3. The Church Doctrine.
180. What is the usage of the word regeneration by our older dogmaticians?
181. How did they use the word conversion?
182. What is the true usage in the strict sense?
183. What does it mean in its active and transitive sense?
184. What is its meaning in the passive sense?
185. What does Hollaz mean by its intransitive sense?
186. What two questions arise in describing the freedom the will?
187. What freedom has the natural man?
188. In what sense is it true that we cannot be converted against our will?
189. Distinguish between regeneration and conversion.
190. Draw a sharp distinction between transitive Conversion and intransitive conversion.
191. What two questions arise in discussing preparation for conversion?
192. What is the view of Hunnius as to what the natural man can do in his preparation?
193. What was the opinion of Musaeus?
194. How was this opposed by the orthodox dogmaticians?
195. In what did this discussion culminate?
196. How did Julius Mueller try to solve the question?
197. In what sense is he synergistic?
198. What position does Thomasius take?
199. What does the Formula of Concord say of the relation of the will to grace?
200. Who begins the saving work of conversion?
201. What does Chemnitz say On this point?
202. When does man begin to co-operate with God?
203. What illustration does Chemnitz use?
204. How does Quenstedt trace the steps of grace in conversion?
205. In what sense is it instantaneous?
206. Show that we can resist prevenient grace.
207. What does Julius Mueller hold?
208. How does Thomasius answer him?
209. How do we understand the old dogmatic formula "In conversion man is merely passive"?
210. How does Quenstedt define conversion?

211. Define conversion in its wide sense.
212. Define conversion in its narrow sense.
213. Define conversion in its special sense.
214. Define conversion in its most special sense.
215. Distinguish between transitive and intransitive conversion.
216. Define more fully intransitive conversion.
217. What is its starting point?
218. How may actual sins be abolished?
219. How does: grace work before conversion, in it, and after it?
220. Define prevenient grace.
221. Define operative grace.
222. Define co-operative grace.
223. Define assisting grace.
224. What does grace affect in conversion?
225. Show that man is passive in conversion.
226. What distinction does Hutter make between the conversion of the unregenerate, of the lapsed, and of the standing?
227. What is the important question at issue?
228. How would you answer it?
229. How does Calovius answer it?
230. What are· the two causes of our conversion?

VI. REPENTANCE.
I. The Scripture Doctrine.
231. With what does conversion begin?
232. What is the negative and what the positive side of conversion?
233. Define penitence.
234. What are the constant demands of the prophets?
235. Show that the New Testament begins with the preaching of repentance.
236. Show that it was a part of the mission of our Lord.
237. Show that it was the substance and aim of the apostolic preaching.
238. Show that it was the great theme of Paul's preaching.
239. Show that God also produces repentance by punishment.
240. Show that repentance is connected with godly sorrow.
241. Define genuine repentance.
2. The Church Doctrine.
1. The Early Church.
242. Trace the corruption of the meaning of penitence.

243. Describe the stations of penitence.

> 2. The Teaching of the Roman Catholic Church,

244. Describe the· three parts of the sacrament of penance.

> 3. Luther and the Lutheran Confessions.

245. How does the Apology present the true view of repentance?

246. Discuss more fully the presentation of the Apology.

247. In what sense does it use the word repentance?

248. How does the Formula of Concord use the word in its narrow sense?

249. Show that the Augsburg Confession uses repentance in the wide sense.

> 4. The Doctrine of our Dogmaticians.

250. How does Hollaz define it?

251. Distinguish between the repentance of those who fall and of those who stand.

252. Draw a distinction between the two parts of repentance.

253. Between what six point does Gerhard draw a distinction?

254. Into what five parts do some divide contrition?

255. What are the objects of contrition?

256. What are the requisites of true contrition?

257. Show that contrition is only a medium of salvation.

258. What are the marks of true contrition?

259. What does the Lutheran Church teach concerning auricular confession?

260. Discuss its evil.

261. Discuss confession in general.

262. What is the teaching of our Church concerning private absolution?

263. State the difference between private confession and private absolution.

264. Why is private absolution a blessing preliminary to communion?

265. What is the Romish doctrine of satisfaction?

266. Show that repentance continues through life.

VII. FAITH.

> I. The Scripture Doctrine.

267. What is the aim of repentance?

268. What is the main element of faith?

269. Discuss the Hebrew, the Greek, the German, and the English meaning of faith.

270. What do we learn from Hebrews 11: 1 as to the meaning of faith?

271. What do we learn from Romans 4:18?

272. What is the usage both in the Old and in the New Testament?

273. On what authority does our faith rest?

274. Explain this more fully.

275. What is the content of our faith?

276. What is the aim of faith?

277. Distinguish in the use of prepositions eis, epi, and en.

278. What is the special character of the eleventh chapter of Hebrews?

279. Illustrate faith by the faith of Abraham.

280. Show that faith is the center of the preaching in the synoptic gospels.

281. Show that Christ is the object of faith.

282. Show that stress is laid on faith in the Sermon on the Mount.

283. What stress is laid on faith in St. John's Gospel?

284. How are the elements of faith depicted?

285. How is the aim of faith represented?

286. How does St. Paul present faith?

287. By what prepositions and in what way is it ordinarily expressed?

288. Show that its true element is trust and confidence.

      2. The Church Doctrine.

289. What is the teaching of Clemens Romanus?

290. Of Ignatius?

291. Of Justin Martyr?

292. Of Augustine?

293. Of Peter Lombard?

294. What distinction did he draw between unformed faith and completely formed faith?

295. What is the teaching of Thomas Aquinas?

296. What does he regard as the object of faith?

297. What distinction does he make between an implicit faith and an explicit faith?

298. Upon what aspect does the Protestant Reformation lay stress?

299. How does the Apology define faith?

300. How does the Formula of Concord define it?

301. Upon what did Luther lay great stress?
302. Show that Luther laid stress on the divine aspect of faith.
303. What does he teach of its relation to repentance?
304. Distinguish between justifying and historical faith.
305. Between abstract faith and incarnate faith.
306. Between true faith and false faith.
307. Show its relation to regeneration in its broad sense, and sanctification.
308. Show that it is the witness and life of works.
309. Show that its power is derived from Christ.
310. Show that Luther lays great stress on the power of faith.
311. Show that the Reformation laid great stress on the true idea of faith.
312. Describe the nature and quality of faith.
313. What are the three elements?
314. Show that trust is the most essential.
315. Show that it is receptive arid operating.
316. Show that we can have a full assurance of God's mercy.
317. Show that Romanism and Lutheranism differ in three points in regard to faith.
318. How does Baier define knowledge?
319. How does Quenstedt define assent?
320. How does Hollaz define confidence?
321. What distinction does Baier make between implicit and explicit faith?
322. What distinction does Hollaz make between general assent and special assent?
323. How does Hollaz define confidence for the essence of faith?
324. What distinction does Hollaz draw between general and special faith?
325. Show that God is the principal efficient cause of saving faith.
326. What is the instrumental cause of faith?
327. How does Hollaz distinguish between direct and dis- cursive faith?
328. How does Hollaz distinguish between dead and living faith?
329. How does Hollaz distinguish between receptive and operative faith?
330. How does Brenz state this?
331. What distinction does Hollaz make between weak and strong faith?

332. What does Chemnitz say?
333. How does Hollaz show that certainty belongs to faith in Christ?
334. What does Quenstedt say of the origin of justifying faith?
335. Of its effects?
336. Of its consequences?
337. Of its reward?
338. Of its relation to virtues?

VIII. JUSTIFICATION.
    1. The Scripture Doctrine.
339. Define justification in general.
340. Show that in the Old Testament the doctrine of justification is already taught.
341. Show that there is a distinction between the Greek usage and the biblical of the word righteousness.
342. What is the signification of righteousness in the gospel?
343. In what epistle is it the leading theme?
344. What do we learn from Rom. 3: 24 and 6: 23?
345. What four questions here come under consideration?
346. Discuss the first question: what is the meaning of the expression to justify?
347. What two things does justification involve?
348. On what is our peace conditioned?
349. What is the condition of justification?
350. What is the nature of true faith that justifies?
351. Show that the three elements of faith must be present in true faith.
352. Show that the power of the true faith is twofold.
353. Show that the Pauline doctrine of justification is also taught in the epistles of the first captivity.
354. Show that there is no contradiction between the doctrinal systems of James and Paul with reference to faith.
    2. The Church Doctrine.
355. Show that the Pauline doctrine was soon lost.
356. Show that there ·was a constant growth of a Pelagianizing error in the Middle Ages.
357. What was the teaching of the period of the Reformation?
358. What is the teaching of the Augsburg Confession?
359. Show that it was the central article of faith.

360. What did Osiander teach?

361. What did Stancarus teach?

362. What did the Formula of Concord teach against both these errorists?

363. What stress does it lay upon the exclusive particles?

364. What is the general statement of the teaching of our dogmaticians?

365. Of what two parts does justification consist?

366. What is the instrumental cause of justification?

367. What is its relation to sanctification?

368. Show that justification is absolutely perfect.

369. Show that it is a source of the deepest assurance.

370. How does Quenstedt define justification?

371. What does Baier say to prove that we are justified by faith?

372. How does Baier prove that justification has a forensic sense?

373. How does Gerhardt prove this?

374. Show that justification does not mean a real and internal change of man.

375. Show that our justification consists of two things.

376. Show that the remission of sins and the imputation of Christ's righteousness are inseparable,

377. In what does the form of imputation consist?

378. Show the reality of the imputation.

379. How does Quenstedt express this?

380. What is the internal cause of our justification?

381. What is the external and meritorious cause?

382. What is the instrumental cause?

383. Distinguish between justification and new obedience.

384. How does Chemnitz express this?

385. What four reasons does Melanchthon give why we should retain the particle gratis?

386. How does Chemnitz express this?

387. What are the effects of justification?

388. What are the properties of justification?

IX. THE MYSTICAL UNION AND ADOPTION.
I. The Scripture Doctrine.

389. Define regeneration in a narrow sense.

390. When does the mystical union begin?

391. What is meant by the nuptial union?

392. What are the means of bestowing it on the part of God?
393. What are the means of receiving it on the part of man?
394. What two extremes does the pure doctrine of the mystery oppose?
395. What is meant by adoption?
396. How is this divine sonship also expressed in Scripture?
397. What special privileges belong to adoption?
398. What Greek word for adoption does St. Paul use?
399. What is its significance in Gal. 4 : 5?
400. How does he use it in Rom. 8: 15, 23?
401. How does he use it in Rom. 9 : 4?
402. How does he use it in Eph. 1: 5?
　　　2. The Church Doctrine.
403. How does Quenstedt state the time of the mystical union?
404. How does he define the mystical union?
405. Give his four proofs of the mystical union.
406. How does he present the difference between the general union with God and the special mystical union?
407. Flow does Hollaz explain the difference?
408. Show that the mystical union is not a substantial one.
409. Show that this mystical union is not a personal one.

X. RENOVATION, SANCTIFICATION, AND GOOD WORKS.
　　　1. The Scripture Doctrine.
410. How does the new life manifest itself?
411. Give the general definition of sanctification.
412. What is its negative aspect and what its positive?
　　　2. The Church Doctrine.
413. Show that the conceptions of justification and sanctification were mingled in the early Church.
414. What was the conception of Augustine?
415. What was taught in the middle ages?
416. What ·was the great task of the Reformation?
417. What was its teaching concerning good works?
418. Why are good works necessary?
419. What is the negative side or renovation?
420. What is the positive side or sanctification?
421. How can the Christian character he developed?
422. Draw a fuller distinction between renovation and sanctification.

423. How does Hollaz draw the distinction?

424. What six-fold difference does Quenstedt make between regeneration and renovation?

425. What is the starting point of renovation?

426. What is the goal of renovation?

427. What is the form. of renovation?

428. Show that renovation and sanctification are progressive.

429. Show that renovation and sanctification admit degrees.

430. What is the efficient cause of sanctification?

431. Show that the regenerate man co-operates with God in the work of sanctification.

432. Define good works.

433. Why are the works of justified man called good?

434. Show that all good works are imperfect.

435. What is their source?

436. Show that the upright works of the unregenerate cannot be called good.

437. How does the Apology characterize spiritually good works?

438. Show that good works should be spontaneous arid free.

439. Show that good works have their reward.

440. How does Quenstedt describe Christian Warfare?

Made in the USA
Columbia, SC
19 February 2018